Stephen Allen

Religion and science

Stephen Allen

Religion and science

ISBN/EAN: 9783337134655

Printed in Europe, USA, Canada, Australia, Japan

Cover: Foto ©Lupo / pixelio.de

More available books at **www.hansebooks.com**

RELIGION AND SCIENCE;

THE

Letters of "Alpha"

ON THE

INFLUENCE OF SPIRIT UPON IMPONDERABLE ACTIENIC MOLECULAR SUBSTANCES,

AND THE

LIFE-FORCES OF MIND AND MATTER.

Embracing a Review

OF THE

ADDRESS OF PROF. JOHN TYNDALL, LL.D., F.R.S., Etc.,

BEFORE THE BRITISH ASSOCIATION AT BELFAST, AUGUST 19, 1874,

WITH ADDITIONAL EVIDENCE, THROUGH THE LAW OF "EVOLUTION," OF THE IMMORTALITY OF THE SOUL, ITS RELATIONS TO PHYSICAL LIFE, AND ACCOUNTABILITY TO THE DEITY.

BY THE AUTHOR OF

"FIBRILIA AND FIBROUS MANUFACTURES," "THE ACTIEN THEORY, AND LETTERS ON A NEWLY DISCOVERED LAW IN PHYSICS, THE ORIGIN OF LIGHT AND HEAT, THE AUTOMATIC FORMATION OF COLOR," Etc.

BOSTON:
JAMES CAMBPELL.
1875.

Entered, according to Act of Congress, in the year 1875,

By STEPHEN M. ALLEN,

In the Office of the Librarian of Congress at Washington.

TO

GEORGE BUCKHAM, Esq.,

THE UNCOMPROMISING SUPPORTER OF RELIGION,

THE FRIEND OF SCIENCE;

AND AN EARNEST BELIEVER THAT TRUTH IN EVERY FORM IS THE HIGHEST

PROMOTER OF

HUMAN KNOWLEDGE AND HAPPINESS,

THROUGH THE INSPIRATIONAL TEACHINGS OF EITHER

SCIENCE OR RELIGION;

THIS VOLUME

𝔍𝔰 𝔑𝔢𝔰𝔭𝔢𝔠𝔱𝔣𝔲𝔩𝔩𝔶 𝔇𝔢𝔡𝔦𝔠𝔞𝔱𝔢𝔡

BY HIS FRIEND,

THE AUTHOR.

CONTENTS.

ESSAY I.
INHERENT RELIGIOUS RIGHTS IN MAN.

MATTER AND SPIRIT: THE QUESTION OF WHICH TAKES PRECEDENCE A VITAL ONE AT THE PRESENT TIME. — WHETHER A SUPREME BEING IS INTENDED TO BE RECOGNIZED BY SCIENTIFIC TEACHERS, OR WHETHER ATHEISM LURKS BENEATH, TO BE PROCLAIMED ON FUTURE OCCASIONS. — MOLECULAR AND ATOMIC MATTER, AND THEIR RELATIONS TO ANIMAL LIFE AND EVOLUTION. — ALL PEOPLE, EITHER SAVAGE OR CIVILIZED, FROM THE BEGINNING OF TIME, HAVE BELIEVED IN SOME SORT OF DEITY, THE IMMORTALITY OF THE SOUL, AND IN REWARDS AND PUNISHMENTS. — LIFE-FORCES IN MATTER BORROW THEIR STRENGTH FROM SPIRIT.

ESSAY II.
RELIGION EVER SUPPORTS SCIENCE.

NEWTON, GOETHE, AND ARISTOTLE. — EDUCATION AND GENERAL EXPERIENCE ENLARGE INSTEAD OF CONTRACT THE MIND FOR THE COMPREHENSION OF SPECIALTIES. — NATURALISM AND THEISM. — GOD IS ALL THINGS IN THEIR IDEA. — LOVE AND PROVIDENCE, LAW AND WISDOM. — IF GOD IS A TRINITY, IN THAT HE IS THE PROTOTYPE OF MAN.

ESSAY III.
SPIRIT AND MATTER.

AN IMPULSE MAY BE INHERENT THROUGH PHYSICAL MAN, AND YET NOT BE MATERIAL BUT SPIRITUAL. — DEITY HARMONIOUS IN HIS WORK. — THE PRIMEVAL MAN. — SELF-CONSCIOUS SPIRITUAL IMPULSE. — THE BRAIN AND INTELLECT BORROW THEIR MOTIVE FORCE FROM SPIRIT. — SOUL AND INTELLECT OF MAN POINT TO PRINCIPLES BEYOND. — WHAT ARE MOLECULES AND ATOMS? — THEIR EXPANSION AND CONTRACTION. — THE SHELL OF MOLECULES THE FOUNDATION OF PHYSICAL ATOMS OR THE SUBSTANCE OF ANIMAL FIBRE.

ESSAY IV.
MATERIAL LIFE-FORCES.

A LARGE MAJORITY OF TRUE SCIENTISTS BELIEVE IN RELIGION. — THE EARTH'S LIGHT AND HEAT. — OLD THEORIES UNREASONABLE AND INCONSISTENT WITH GOD'S LAW OF USES. — NO REASON OR PROOF OF THE ASSUMPTIONS OF LATE ASTRONOMERS THAT THE SUN GIVES OUT THE HEAT ESTIMATED BY THEM. — LIGHT MAY BE GENERATED IN THE ATMOSPHERE AS HEAT AND COLD MAY BE PRODUCED. — COLOR A CONDITION, NOT A FIXED LAW.

ESSAY V.
MECHANICAL EVOLUTION.

LIFE-FORCE OF MOLECULAR MOTION. — SPIRIT THE PRIMARY AUTHOR. — DEMOCRITUS NO GUIDE TO SCIENCE THOUGH BELIEVING IN A DEITY. — EPICURUS A BETTER TEACHER, THOUGH MUCH DEFAMED IN HIS SUPPOSED PRINCIPLES. — HE ADORED THE GODS, BUT IN THE ORDINARY FASHION. — LUCRETIUS AND THE MECHANICAL SHOCK OF ATOMS. — HIS IDEA OF INTELLIGENT DESIGN IN THE CONSTITUTION OF NATURE. — DEMOCRITUS' IDEA, THAT FROM NOTHING COMES NOTHING. — THE CREATION BY BOTH DIVINE AND HUMAN CALCULATION MUST HAVE HAD A BEGINNING.

ESSAY VI.
TRUTH AND SOPHISTRY.

SPIRIT OF THE MIDDLE AGES. — THE SPECIALTIES OF SOCRATES, ARISTOTLE, AND OTHERS. — SCIENCE NOT RETARDED BY RELIGION. — FALL OF ROME AND OTHER CITIES ATTRIBUTED TO MATERIAL AND NOT SPIRITUAL CAUSES. — ERRORS OF SCIENTISTS OF THE PRESENT AGE.

ESSAY VII.
SCIENCE AND THE MIDDLE AGES.

PROFESSOR TYNDALL'S COMPLAINT OF THE MIDDLE AGES. — A DRAWBACK TO SCIENTIFIC PROGRESS. — ONE THOUSAND YEARS AS EVENTFUL AS ANY OTHER EQUAL LENGTH OF TIME IN THE HISTORY OF THE WORLD. — ALEXANDER THE GREAT TO BELISARIUS. — PARTITION OF THE ROMAN EMPIRE TO THE ESTABLISHMENT OF THE GREEK EMPIRE. — EGYPT, SYRIA, PERSIA, ROME. — THE GAULS, CELTS, AND BRITONS. — SCIENCE DID NOT PERISH IN ROME THROUGH RELIGIOUS FANATICISM. — THE ROMANS ESTABLISHED SLAVERY. — OXFORD AND CAMBRIDGE INCORPORATED.

ESSAY VIII.
ATOMIC CONCEPTIONS.

PROTAGORAS THE ATHEISTIC SOPHIST. — STRAIN UPON THE HUMAN MIND. — GEORDANO BRUNO BURNED FOR HERESY. — WANT OF CHARITY IN SECTARIANISM. — CHRISTENDOM SICK OF THE SCHOOL OF PHILOSOPHY. — MATERIALISTS DISGUSTED WITH THEIR OWN WORK. — CRAVING FOR UNITY. — UNITY OF PHYSICAL FORCES. — A RELIGIOUS SPIRIT MADE PLACE FOR COPERNICUS, GASSENDI, AND ATOMIC CONSTRUCTIONS.

ESSAY IX.
MOLECULAR CONSTRUCTION.

THE CONNECTION BETWEEN SPIRIT AND MATTER. — ELECTRIC TELEGRAPH. — BISHOP BUTLER'S VIEWS. — WHY WILL VAPOR FLOAT IN THE ATMOSPHERE? — WHY IS THE THEORY OF UNDULATION CREDITED TO YOUNG? — WHY ARE CORPUSCLES USED FOR ILLUSTRATING NEWTON'S THEORY OF LIGHT WHEN HE USED THEM ONLY TO ILLUSTRATE COLORS? — OLD CONCEPTIONS RELAXED. — DARWIN'S ORIGIN OF SPECIES. — MOLESCHOTT'S VIEWS OF THOUGHT AND MATTER. — THE PRACTICAL MAN THE WORK OF A DIVINE LAW. — FATE HAS WEAK POINTS.

ESSAY X.
SCIENCE AND SOCIOLOGY.

THE PRESENT A GENERATION PECULIAR TO ITSELF. — THE PRINCIPLES OF EVOLUTION HAVE THEIR INFLUENCE IN FORMATION OF MAN OF HIS ESPECIAL DAY. — THE PEOPLE THE REAL SUPPORT OF SCIENCE. — MAJORITY OF MUSCULAR FORCES THE MAJORITY OF NUMBERS. — THE SPIRITUAL AND PHYSICAL TYPE OF MAN. — PSYCHO-ANIMAL LIFE PROGRESSIVELY REGENERATIVE.

ESSAY XI.
SEISMIC AND MENTAL ENERGIES.

SPIRITUAL AND ETHEREAL IDEA HAS PRECEDENCE. — A BELIEF IN SCIENCE AND RELIGION. — THE DARK AGES HELD A CURTAIN OVER THE PAST. — THE END OF PROFESSOR TYNDALL'S ADDRESS. — THE END NOT YET, SAY THE TENS OF THOUSANDS WHO HAVE READ IT. THE MENTAL ENERGIES AND REVELATIONS OF OUR OWN DAY HAVE BEEN GENERAL AND DIFFUSIVE. — THEORIES OF HUMBOLDT

AND HERSCHEL. — LIGHT AND HEAT AS SUCH MAY NOT EMANATE FROM THE SUN. — AN OPEN POLAR SEA. — SCIENCE UNEMOTIONAL MAY APPROACH THE FOOTSTOOL OF THE THRONE, BUT RELIGION ALONE, THE SOUL OF SCIENCE, CAN DRINK IN THE GLEAMS OF IT DIVINE EXISTENCE.

ESSAY XII.
CREATION OF THE UNIVERSE.

AN IMPULSE OF DEITY, INHERENT THROUGH ITS OWN ENTITY, CREATED AND INSPIRED THE WORLD OF SPIRIT. — IMPONDERABLE MATERIAL FORCES FOLLOWED. — PONDERABLE MOLECULES, ATOMIC AND NEBULOUS MATTER. — ELECTRICITY AND MAGNETISM. — AGGREGATION OF MATTER. — SEISMIC FORCES AND UPHEAVALS. — ANIMAL LIFE. — MOUNTAINS CRUMBLE TO DUST, OCEAN BEDS ARE RAISED. — THE BIRTH OF WORLDS BEGINS. — A NEW LIFE, AND MAN A HUMAN SOUL APPEARS.

PREFACE.

The following pages, mostly compiled from the letters of "Alpha," written for the "Boston Daily Transcript," and quotations from distinguished writers upon the subjects therein treated, are intended to place before the world, in a concise form, some of the many logical arguments easily understood by the common mind, against the advancement of Atheism apparent in late scientific teachings. The intention of the author is further to show that "life-forces" in matter may be accounted for much earlier than the present claims of scientists, even without giving them separate independence of motion, or a "conscious existence," except through "spirit" emanating from Deity. In the choice of quotations the author has abstained from the use of sectarian dogmas, and to a certain extent has brought in the expressed views of different writers of many religious denominations, who speak for themselves. The arguments are intended, so far as they go, to show that Material as well as Mental and Social Science, is dependent upon "spirit" for its active creative force, and that the latter originates with God alone; that illustrative Science, as taught at the present day, when properly demonstrated, by no means disproves the immortality of the soul, its accountability to God, or the necessities of a religious life, but on the contrary in all its lessons points to a perfect harmony between Religion and Science, and a higher and independent life beyond the grave. The teachings of late scientists in Europe would, if taken literally, contradict this fact, and set the human mind adrift upon a shoreless ocean of doubt and conflict, where comparatively few in the past have ever found a haven of even imaginary rest. The author assumes, through the use of his own and quoted ideas, that much that is claimed as practical Science is erroneous, and that its propagators are as much dogmatists as have been some teachers of Religion in the past, and that many of the theories of Science that from time to time have been raised have entirely fallen. It is presumed that the present is no exception, and that some of the most glowing of scientific dogmas, now uppermost, will share a like fate with those in generations gone by. We hold that the natural laws and influences of Religion ever have and ever will be the true nursery of human progress, and that this spirit in every age has been the great sustaining force which held up and developed Science. In behalf of this opinion it may be assumed that the Religion of the Middle Ages did not destroy, but did much to sustain, that spark of Science, which, since fanned by united and diffusive intelligence, has grown to be the wonder of the world. We shall be reminded that the classic cities of the East, once supposed by their world-wise and credulous builders to be the proof of the highest civilization, and their inhabitants, the patrons of all knowledge and greatness, if not goodness, slowly but ceaselessly crumbled to dust, which now, in common with that of their wisest men, is scattered upon the desert, the abode of the "savage and the brute." But it will be in vain that material scientists claim the downfall of these cities of the East through a religious faith, or even religious fanaticism. How obvious the proof to every mind that it was "Materialism" and not "Religion" that laid waste the palaces of kings and nobles, and levelled them with the earth! It was an assumed intellectuality, a fictitious control of matter through mind, that really disintegrated the fabled walls of Science, and Spirituality only waked too late to find them mere dust. The author may be excused in this connection with the introduction of extensive individual ideas and theories on some of the scientific points in discussion, which at first sight may appear to contradict some principles in Science which seem to be, but are not yet, "fixed." While he is a believer in Science he is also a believer in Religion, in which all are interested; and where theories, new or old, can be set up to establish a union of these principles it may be legitimate to do so. The author is well aware that it is unusual for laymen of a scientific or religious faith to engage in controversies of this magnitude, which should have, and be able to draw support from, the highest professional knowledge and skill. But in the end, if it should be found that this small contribution is equivalent to the "widow's mite," he will have the satisfaction of doing something for the cause of Religion to gain the Master's approval. Should there be one new principle developed in Science at the same time, he feels that the work of years is not lost, and that the hours withdrawn from a laborious business life may prove compensative, and though of small service to the student of nature, yet with no injury to the professional scientist or clergyman, whose province may seem to have been invaded.

S. M. A.

BOSTON, November 1, 1874.

INTRODUCTION.

"ACTIEN" is a new word used in illustration of a theory of light, heat, and color, published in various forms by the author in 1860. The need of a representative word to precede *actin*, the Greek word for rays, was to establish and illustrate a parent principle or root. It was coined because no existing word exactly expressed the idea intended to be illustrated. It would be improper to use the word *actin*, which means rays only, and which carries with it no idea of the origin, substance, or composition of rays, the molecules of which might be of different characters; neither would it be justifiable to say "actinic rays," as some scientists have done, for this would be making two words of the Greek root and the English word meaning precisely the same thing, neither of which, used alone or together, would give an idea of the essence, origin, or composition of the ray itself. Actien, then, is the first positive, physical principle in nature, and is the essence, composition, or parent of rays; and actienic rays are those peculiar rays of which "Actien" is the base, composition, or support.

The actien theory recognizes a universe of spirit in the creation and support of all things, — soul, mind, and matter. The formula would be, first, Deity, with all His attributes; second, Spirit, with its inherent Divine energies; third, Soul, through its conscious connection with ponderable and imponderable matter. Succeeding these, two original, procreative, physical principles follow, working through or containing within themselves positive and negative forces, from and through the united action of which all material molecular, atomic, or the highest ethereal imponderable molecular substance is produced. The first of these is "Action," the active, and the second is "Ether," the negative principle, and from the impact, union, force, and action of these, through Divine impulse, all that we know of earth, water, gases, air, electricity, magnetism, the solar, astral, and celestial systems are produced, each central sun, when aggregated, throwing off its surplus Actienic forces for other planetary creations. Taking the solar system as an illustration, "Action," or the positive principle, would be defined as a primary element or fluid, emanating from the sun, which, in passing through "Ether," the negative force of intervening space, produces the effects above enumerated in molecular atomic nebulus or planetary construction. The first flows from the sun, either in all directions through the solar system, or in concentrated rays exclusively upon the planets of its creation, in general, straight lines, not necessarily carrying either light or heat as it travels, by undulating vibrations through space. These elements are generated principally within the circle of the atmosphere surrounding the planets when the fluid pervades the same, the impulse and contact instantly causing a combustion, producing angular luminous waves, and all the changes which we enjoy in their various phases, including light and heat, together with electricity and magnetism, in the forms of which we know their use and power, with many other conditions existing in the chemical and geological combinations which surround us on every hand, numerous forms of which are beyond our present comprehension.

These fluids positive and negative thus comprehend the origin of the whole planetary system,—the solid emanating from a moleculous, atomic, or analogous condition, similar to what is now supposed to form nebulous aggregations, or *cometary systems*, followed by condensation and consolidation, until all the forms of planetary matter are created of which we have any knowledge, the bodies graduating in their orbit according to density for the time being, in the absence of other influences, the eccentricity of the same diminishing as the density of the planet increases.

The electric and magnetic fluids, which at first sight seem to be the most subtile of all acknowledged agents, at the present time are not in reality primary elements, neither do they contain independent life-forces, as they exist, but rather are creations from powers more subtile than they, which of themselves are primary in the creation of physical matter, and from which both electricity and magnetism, the gases and atmosphere, are created through molar friction, undulation, and contact with the primal properties of the aggregating earth and its increasing atmospheric surroundings. From the union of this actienic element and its negative, proceed all the physical consequences connected with the origin, subsequent changes, or present condition of the earth, which would be observed in its annual passage round the sun, or its diurnal revolutions on its own axis.

The form of combination and combustion of actien with other substances is instantly checked and relaxed, and the elements of force lie in a semi-dormant state, when any physical obstacle of greater density than the atmosphere shall interpose to break its currents directly towards any part of the surface of the earth on which we may stand. Thus, when the sun shall have sunk behind the western horizon, the line of the same interposes an obstacle in the way of a free traverse of the fluid towards a more eastern point of the earth's surface, and darkness in its various forms intervene.

The establishment of these laws would account for

the difference in temperature and molecular character of the atmosphere between the poles and the equator, and the tropical and polaric influences of each, as now understood. It would also account for the aurora borealis, the rainbow, the emission, reflection, refraction, and undulation of light, the temporary condition and forces of heat and cold, and the automatic formation of color.

The molecular changes in the decomposition of "Actien" and "Ether" within our atmosphere above the horizon, while the sun has set below it in the evening, or above the sun before it rises in the morning, produces rays, when carefully examined, similar to those we know as the zodiacal lights; and the same forces, penetrating the atmosphere of the pole, while under the peculiar influence of the recontact or impact of the magnetic and electric currents as they sink through the pole, or may rise up through the atmosphere on their return to the equator in combustion with the new volume of actien precipitated upon that part of the pole still subject to sunlight, with the influences of an open polar sea upon crystallized, vaporous, atomic matter, would account for all the colors and flashes which we often behold so beautifully displayed in that region. The same theory would explain the true character of phosphorescent light, and the luminous tails of comets.

Ordinary light, heat, and color all find their support in the combustion of actien and ether, with some kind of an atmosphere, without which they could not of themselves exist.

The Ether of space has been variously defined for a century past. The author of the Actien theory does not attempt to give it any new properties, unless it be an original negative molar force filling all space, in and through which Actien is a positive working agent, causing all its undulations; the form of the waves sharpening at their crests as combustion increases in the atmosphere, and light is emitted and reflected from wave to wave in lines corresponding with their angle of incidence. The primal actienic force, from its first spirit impulse restless and pungent, produces, as a result, new molecular and corpuscular formations of various kinds at every step, which become aggregated and are subject not only to the original Actienic and Etheric forces, but other new ones generated through evolution, forming other physical conglomerate properties.

Whether the principles of Actien and Ether, before their first impulse, have separate positions in space, held asunder in the main by their respective specific gravities or attracting properties, or whether they exist together through all space, only separated by the individual difference of their force and character, does not matter. It is enough that they exist. Whether the resultant molecules are ponderable or imponderable, solid or hollow, lie side by side or are impelled by expansion and contraction in volumes, from independent location, it is quite certain that they are antagonistic to each other when in motion, and are constantly at war, — the result of which is the creation of a new ponderable molecular and atomic substance, the integration of matter, and the formation of worlds.

RELIGION AND SCIENCE.

ESSAY I.

INHERENT RELIGIOUS RIGHTS.

THE religious world has just cause for special and energetic criticism of recently published scientific ideas and opinions of Professor Tyndall. The question, whether "matter" or "spirit" takes precedence in the constitution and government of man, is especially vital at the present time. The well-being of humanity becomes a stupendous question, when through it we ask whether the recognized principles of Christianity, with reverence and allegiance to Deity, shall be held first and uppermost; or whether Science, as revealed through physical evolution, will explain and should govern the emotional consciousness of a "spiritual power," influencing and controlling man in his relations to himself and his God.

The public mind now asks whether the teachings of the learned professor, so widely diffused and being felt by millions, are intended to recognize a "Supreme Being" in the construction and government of the universe; or whether infidelity and atheism are lurking beneath, at some future time to be openly proclaimed on the wings of some new discovery in

Physics, teaching material existence through unconscious evolutions of matter.

In the paper read by Professor Tyndall, at Belfast, in August, 1874, before the British Association for the Advancement of Science, through a long historical and metaphysical harangue he seems to studiously avoid recognizing any creative power except in and through matter, or that arising under material laws. This furnishes sufficient excuse for every lay or professional scientist who believes in a Supreme Being, every merchant or artisan who is conscious of a moral force stimulating his efforts to aid himself and his fellow-man, and every teacher of religious faith who recognizes a trinity and harmony connected and pervading the whole physical, intellectual, and moral world, — to combat, with all his powers, a doctrine inconsistent alike with the creation of physical matter, the revelation and continuity of spiritual existence, or their united power and force.

It will be remembered by the intelligent reader that about two years ago Professor Tyndall " respectfully proposed or assented to test the relative merit of human prayer, and its efficacy when brought in direct juxtaposition with or arrayed against the highest medical skill." " Two large wards belonging to one hospital were designated as the field of operation, — prayer alone to be employed in one of them, and in the other medical treatment was to be administered agreeably with the best-known science and practice of the schools."

Material demonstrations have not been recognized by any class of religionists as evidence of the highest spiritual communion with God, nor have the answers given to their aspiring, prayerful souls always been physically demonstrated. The highest and most satisfactory assurances of an answer to prayer are often through the "still, small voice" which gives rest and strength to the soul, with a peace resulting beyond a possibility of description through words, but fortifying the mind against the threatened dangers and sufferings arising through the ills of daily life.

Under these circumstances, Professor Tyndall must not blame his friends or the world for questioning the logic, while acknowledging the ingenuity, displayed in his last great effort; neither must he be surprised if thousands of students lose confidence in many of his accustomed demonstrations of science, which heretofore they have received as truth from a teacher whose heart and aim they have not doubted, but whose late writings seem inconsistent with the rule of life, its duties and accomplishments, to which they have been educated, — the spirit of which, they believe, is prompted through Revelation from Deity itself.

From the earliest ages of which we have any account, as well as from prehistoric ages, from which, with Professor Tyndall, we may claim a direct line of continuity, every people, whether savage or civilized, have believed in and worshipped some sort of a Deity. This Principle, however vaguely comprehended or described, they ever considered superior to themselves, the acknowledged creator of all things, either in the heavens above or the earth beneath, and to which they were accountable, and by whom they were rewarded or punished, here or hereafter, according to their works. In this, too, they have recognized a spiritual as well as a material existence, and that the former survived the dissolution of the body. This feeling and belief has not been confined exclusively to any class or condition of men, whether learned or unlearned, bond or free. In the lowest type of devotional conception and accountability, there has been apparent the germ of a sentiment and belief, commensurate and equivalent, so far as that light extended, to what is known in the most civilized portions of the world as Christianity.

All knowledge pertaining to life, to religion, or to the Deity must have existed before any written record we possess; and the impulse of the scribes who made that record will be found as clearly inspirational and spiritual, when working through the minds of the authors, as the steam-engine, electric telegraph, or galvanic battery of to-day proves the pre-existence and mental effort of artisans or handiworkers of a past generation. The impulse to study, to learn, and to produce ever has been and ever will be of divine origin. The published vital principles of revealed religion are held to be but a few thousand years old, yet they must have existed and worked from the creation of the world. Long before the Mosaic Code or the New Testament was written, these teachings were constantly revealing, but did not create, a law, and opened it as a special revelation to the mind of man. Religion, too, is as simple as it is natural to the human soul, receiving its emotional forces from Deity, and running back again to its Maker laden with thanksgivings and praise, and ever yearning for new light and greater progress in all that pertains to life's duties and knowledge.

The rapid progress made through old opinions are shown in Professor Tyndall's address, but not clearer than in the teachings of the clergy throughout Christendom. Science has always had its votaries, and Religion good workers, outside of professional life, or the pale of the Church, which proves that it is not teaching alone that inspires confidence in either.

During the last twenty-five years many have carefully observed the rapid strides of Materialism as opposed to Religion, and have sought in a measure to study and substantiate parallels to the new theories propagated by scientists, with a view sometimes to show their fallacy by giving other reasons than those shown by them for proving the phenomena of physical evolution. The result of this has been the building up, in some minds at least, of a settled belief that there exists more error, if not dogmatism, among scientists, than the Church has produced for the last three hundred years. The result of these investigations has been the substitution of new but apparently consistent theories of the forces, assumed by scientists for molecular matter, which would even go beyond theirs in creating animal life, yet claim no existence, independent of the great motor, Spirit, emanating from God.

M. Wurtz, in his address to the French Association for the Promotion of Science, recently held at Lille, discoursed extensively on the "theory of atoms," and their relation to the general conception of the universe. He does not speak altogether confidently of his opinions, and adds, "We must be careful how we hastily formulate the judgment, that, because to our limited vision all is perfect and clear, the doctrines we enunciate are inevitably right, and those of our opponents lamentably and unalterably wrong." At the same time that M. Wurtz is trying to enlighten the citizens of France on physical construction without ignoring a living faith in God, M. Dupanloup, Bishop of Orleans, is making efforts to increase religious faith by the canonization of Joan of Arc.

Professor Tyndall goes a step beyond M. Wurtz in atoms, and arrives at molecules as the primary constituent of our existence, molecular force becoming structural, and the agency "by which both plants and animals are built up." He does not enlighten us from what source the original impulse springs, but from inference we may judge it is spontaneous, reacting upon itself.

These ideas differ widely from those of religious exponents, as do those published by different scientists regarding their own respective theories. The rapidity of advancement is as marked as those used in the exposition of the law of Physics. The simple-minded devotee to either Science or Religion finds as much as he can do to keep pace with the essential teachings of either; and but for the consciousness and faith within him, that there is a God who not only creates but controls all things, he would sometimes fear his opportunities were not sufficient, while attending to his daily duties, to inform himself, through the multiplication of such teachings, of the observance of the physical or spiritual laws necessary to secure his own well-being.

Professor Tyndall's sympathy with Lange in his "History of Materialism" is unequivocally expressed in his late address, though he claims him as a non-materialist, while Democritus is his favorite early delineator. He runs through the list of ancient as well as modern philosophers, selecting from one a point of illustration used for his purposes, from another an opposite one of contradiction, but all pointing in the direction of Materialism, as containing the organizing forces of human existence, and denying the greatest of all principles, Spiritual Entity.

There is nothing in the calling of either clergy or scientist that need bias the mind against the truth, whatever it may be, whether it is the revelation of Religion or Science. It may truly be said that man has never existed without a " science," or some scientific belief, independent of his spiritual life or duty, and that in his nature he holds this principle in great reverence.

In the evolutions of life, there have been paroxysms of "idea" showing themselves both in the principles of Religion and Science, and we are passing through one of these — and perhaps the greatest the world ever knew — at the present time. In epochs of this kind there is often much said inadvertently by teachers that is not meant, and much of that which is meant is often misunderstood. This, it seems, is particularly true in regard to the teachings of some of the most distinguished European *savans*, including Professor Tyndall. His revision of the Belfast Address, with explanations, would at first sight relieve the public from some anxiety; what he dropped from the first report, and added to the last, places it in a somewhat different light, and renders it capable of a different possible construction: yet, after all, its line of argument is materiality as against spirituality.

"The only true remedy," says James Martineau, "for the dark infidelity and cold materialism that threatens the utter destruction of the religious life in a large portion of the people, is to give them a living faith, — true to the conscience, true to the intellect, true to the realized science of the age."

A public teacher of principles, be they scientific or religious, gains nothing for the force of his arguments by mysticism. Students of every kind of life's teachings feel safer to learn, so far as they may be able, the destiny of a voyage before they set out, and they certainly have a right to know the qualifications, or at least the intentions, of their commander. It seems singular that Prof. Tyndall is willing to leave the world in doubt for a moment as to whether he believes, or does not believe, in a Deity.

Bacon does not deny that science and philosophy, failing in extent and comprehensiveness, may incline to atheism. Our modern scientists leave out of their reckoning those facts of Spiritualism which Bacon knew, and which guarded him from limiting his faith in Deity to deductions from second causes.

It is but just to Professor Tyndall to add, that in the preface of his corrected address he says, "The facts of religious feeling are to me as certain as the facts of Physics." He continues:—

"So likewise as regards a resolution recently passed by the Presbytery of Belfast, in which Professor Huxley and myself are spoken of as 'ignoring the existence of God, and advocating pure and simple Materialism.' Had the possessive pronoun 'our' preceded 'God,' and had the words 'what we consider' preceded 'pure,' this statement would have been objectively true; but to make it so this qualification is required.

"In connection with the charge of Atheism, I would make one remark: Christian men are proved by their writings to have their hours of weakness and of doubt, as well as their hours of strength and of conviction; and men like myself share, in their own way, these variations of mood and tense. Were the religious views of many of my assailants the only alternative ones, I do not know how strong the claims of the doctrine of 'Material Atheism' upon my allegiance might be. Probably they would be very strong. But as it is, I have noticed during years of self-observation that it is not in hours of clearness and vigor that this doctrine commends itself to my mind; that in the presence of stronger and healthier thought it ever dissolves and disappears, as offering no solution of the mystery in which we dwell, and of which we form a part."

These admissions do but very little, however, towards liberalizing his address, in any spiritual sense, and still leaves it open to the imputation of high atheistic tendencies.

Professor Tyndall says: —

"The principles enunciated by Democritus reveal

his uncompromising antagonism to those who deduced the phenomena of nature from the caprices of the gods. They are briefly these: 1. From nothing comes nothing. Nothing that exists can be destroyed. All changes are due to the combination and separation of molecules. 2. Nothing happens by chance. Every occurrence has its cause, from which it follows by necessity. 3. The only existing things are the atoms and empty space; all else is mere opinion. 4. The atoms are infinite in number and infinitely various in form; they strike together, and the lateral motion and whirlings which thus arise are the beginnings of worlds. 5. The varieties of all things depend upon the varieties of their atoms, in number, size, and aggregation. 6. The soul consists of fine, smooth, round atoms, like those of fire. These are the most mobile of all. They interpenetrate the whole body, and in their motions the phenomena of life arise. The first five propositions are a fair general statement of the atomic philosophy, as now held. As regards the sixth, Democritus made his fine, smooth atoms do duty for the nervous system, whose functions were then unknown. The atoms of Democritus are individually without sensation; they combine in obedience to mechanical laws; and not only organic forms, but the phenomena of sensation and thought, are the result of their combination."

To this doctrine we object, and propose in opposition another formula we think more consonant with the divine origin of things and the opinions of man, and which do not conflict with Science or Religion: —

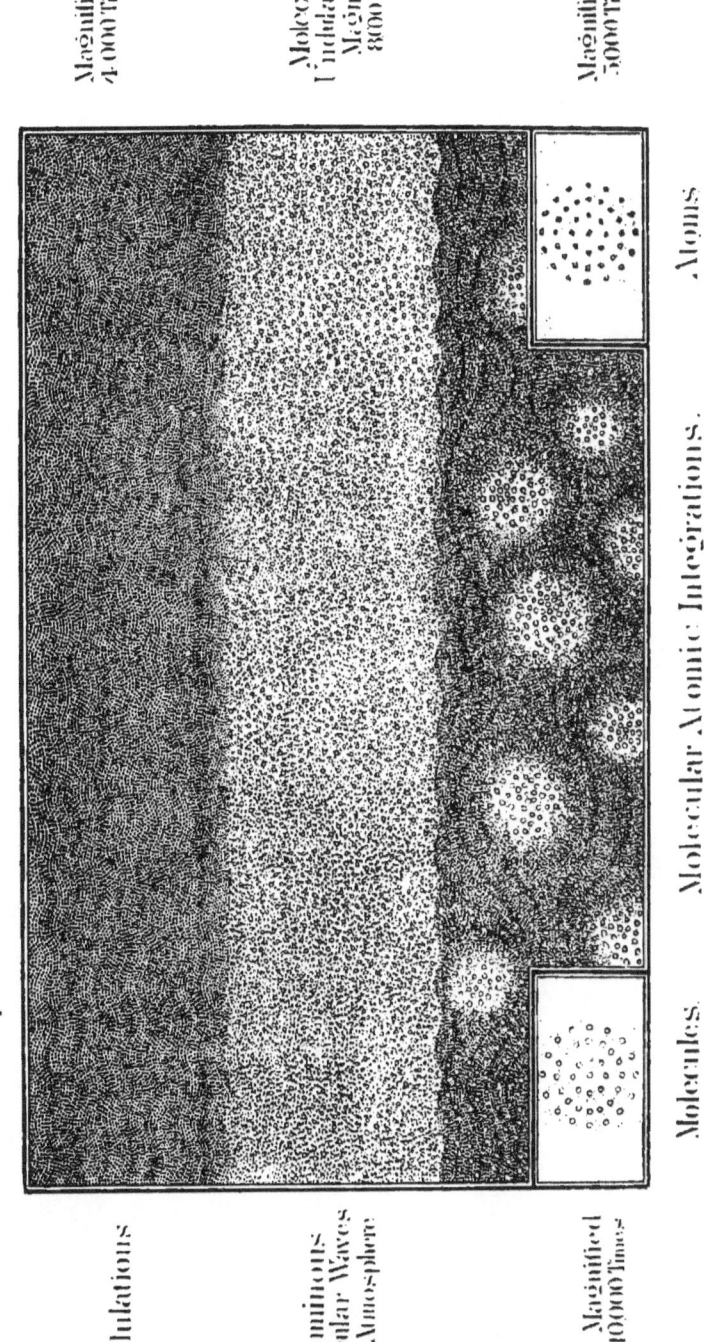

First.	DEITY — ATTRIBUTES.
Second.	WILL — MOTION.
Third.	SPIRIT — SOUL.
*Fourth.**	ACTIEN — ETHER.
Fifth.	ELECTRICITY — MAGNETISM.
Sixth.	MOLECULES — ATOMS.
Seventh.	HEAT — COLD.
Eighth.	ATTRACTION — REPULSION.
Ninth.	INTEGRATION — DISINTEGRATION.
Tenth.	LIFE — DEATH.
Eleventh.	LIGHT — COLOR.

---

* Preface. Actien Theory.

ESSAY II.

RELIGION SUPPORTS SCIENCE.

In generalizing the experiences of Aristotle, Newton, and Goethe, Professor Tyndall infers that their characters as specialists is not as strong as though they were less versatile in their talents and works. In the experience of the world this has not been proven with regard to Religion, except whenever that subject alone has been the specialty. It is a universal truth that talent, education, and general experience have ever enlarged and liberalized the religious idea in man instead of contracting it, and the man with the greatest natural ability, and who has learned and taught Philosophy in an enlarged sphere of action through a long life, has been the better Christian, as well as scientist, and the most liberal in his teachings. This was the case with all three of the above named, and is especially true of Newton. The faults found with Newton's scientific illustrations were not his own, but belonged to those who undertook to interpret them for the world, and who in some cases did it wrongly. The controversy between the ideas of Goethe and Newton grew entirely out of this fact. Newton's definition of light and color had been, and is, wrongly quoted in text-books. These quotations were not received as true by Goethe, and he not only combated them, but went extensively into the study and illustration of the principles governing color, and wrote a book on the subject. It does not appear that Goethe ever discovered these errors in quotation.

The Address at Belfast has probably made more excitement, not only in the religious but in the moral world, than any other of Professor Tyndall's efforts. The press throughout Christendom has been filled with criticism; and it is a mark of the distinguished ability of the learned *savant* that the world is looking down upon him with a stronger individual eye than is at present directed towards any living being, be he prince or king, statesman or scientist. A correspondent, in speaking of Professor Tyndall's ideas, says:—

"That the Address strongly smacks of Materialism no one can gainsay. But that Materialism is capable of solving the problem or philosophy of life, or that it is capable of satisfying all the longings of man's nature, the deeper and diviner elements of his being, the vast majority of enlightened humankind utterly deny.

"Concerning the origin of life, he is in accord with other renowned English scientists,—Darwin, Huxley, Wallace, and Spencer. He traces all the species back to one primordial form, resolves all substantial things into molecules, the universe itself being but a combination of the same ultimate atoms. There is but one God, and Matter is his prophet. He says, 'Abandoning all disguise, the confession I feel bound to make is that . . . I discern in that matter which we in our ignorance, and notwithstanding our professed reverence for its Creator, have hitherto covered with opprobrium, *the promise and potency of every form and quality of life'!*"

Rev. Joseph Cook, of Boston, says:—

"Tyndall's effort is to change the definition of matter. Of the many forms of Materialism, his coincides nearest with a tendency which has been gathering strength among physicists for the last hundred years, to deny that there are two substances in the universe, matter and mind, with opposite qualities, and to affirm that there is but one substance, matter, itself possessed of two sets of properties, or of a physical side and a spiritual side, making up a double-faced unity. This is precisely the Materialism of Professor Bain of Aberdeen, and of Professor Huxley; and its numerous supporters in England, Scotland, and Germany are fond of proclaiming that among metaphysicians as well as among physiologists, it is the growing opinion; and that the arguments to prove the existence of two substances have now entirely lost their validity, and are no longer compatible with ascertained science and clear thinking.

"Tyndall's speculations as to matter are simply an extension of the hypothesis of evolution, according to the scientific doctrine of uniformity, from the known to the unknown. Back to a primordial germ, Darwin is supposed by Tyndall to have traced all organization; back to the properties of unorganized matter in a primordial nebula, Tyndall now traces that germ. Evolution explains everything since the germ. Evolution must be applied to explain as much as possible before the germ. So far as we can test her processes by observation and experiment, Nature is known to proceed by the method of evolution; where we cannot test her processes, analogy requires that we should suppose that she proceeds by the same method.

"As all the organizations now or in past time on the earth were potentially in the primordial germ, so that germ was potentially in the unorganized particles of the primordial star-dust; in other words, there was latent in matter, from the first, the power to evolve organization, thought, emotion, and will. Where matter obtained this power, or whether matter is self-existent, Physical Science has no means of determining. In the evolution of the universe from a primordial haze of matter, possessing both physical and spiritual properties, there has been no design, other than that implied in the original constitution of the molecular particles. Of course, it is utterly futile to oppose these views as self-contradictory in the light of the established definition of matter."*

Dr. McCosh, of Princeton, N. J., says:—

"There were whole departments of Philosophy, running back 2,500 years, comprising the greatest minds of all ages, who have recognized an intelligent designing Cause back of nature, and whom Professor Tyndall wholly ignores."

Dr. Miner, of Boston, in a sermon preached in the Church of the Divine Paternity in New York, "com-

---

* A paper read before the Ministers' Meeting at the Congregational House, Boston, Oct. 5, 1874.

bated with learning and eloquence the assumption that life, in all its multifarious forms, is evolved from the inherent properties of matter, and argued that above and beyond all physical forms and manifestations there is a spiritual intelligence of which matter is only the medium, the whole universe, as the term implies, displaying a unity of design which cannot be accounted for on any hypothesis of the tendency to development which is claimed to exist in primary matter."

In "True Christian Religion" (33 and 47, VI), Swedenborg says: —

"The common idea is that, because what is finite does not comprehend what is infinite, finite things cannot be receptacles of the infinite. But from those things which are said in my works concerning the creation, it is evident that God *first made his infinity finite by substances emitted from himself*, from which exists his proximate encompassing sphere, which makes the sun of the spiritual world; and that afterwards, by means of that sun, he perfected other encompassing spheres, even to the last, which consists of things quiescent; and that *thus, by means of degrees, he made the world finite more and more*. . . . The universe is a work continent of divine love, divine wisdom and uses, and thus altogether a work coherent from firsts to lasts."

Swedenborg also teaches that there are three natures, or degrees of life, in man, — the natural, the spiritual, and the celestial; and that in the celestial, men do not reason about the truth: they see it, because it is a *possession*.

Hegel calls the idea of the Trinity the "pivot of the world."

According to Schelling, God is the perfect spirit in three forms, and the true idea of God is a union of Naturalism and Theism. "Naturalism," he says, "seeks to conceive of God as ground of the world (immanent), while Theism would view him as the world's cause (transcendent); the true course is to unite both determinations. God is at the same time ground and cause.

"It no way contradicts the conception of God to affirm that, so far as he reveals himself, he develops himself from himself, advancing from the imperfect to the perfect; the imperfect is in fact the perfect itself, only in a state of becoming. It is necessary that this becoming should be by stages, in order that the fulness of the perfect may appear on all sides. If there were no obscure ground, no nature, no negative principle in God, we could not speak of a consciousness of God.

"So long as the God of modern Theism remains the simple essence which ought to be purely essential, but which in fact-is without essence, so long as an actual twofoldness is not recognized in God, and a limiting and denying energy (a nature, a negative principle) is not placed in opposition to the extending and affirming energy in God, so long will Science be entitled to make its denial of a personal God. It is universally and essentially impossible to conceive of a Being with consciousness which has not been brought into limit by some denying energy within himself, — as universally and essentially impossible as to conceive of a circle without a centre.

"The fulness of God's being cannot be contained in an abstract unity, and yet his absolute personality *must have unity for its fundamental attribute. The conception of the triune God furnishes us with the sole bridge that can fill up the breach between God and the world.*"

"If we separate," says Vera, "substantially and absolutely, God and the world, we do not only impair and curtail the being of the world, but that of God also. We curtail the being of the world by separating it from its principle; we curtail the being of God by admitting that the substance of the world is independent of God, and consequently by admitting two absolute substances. And the *creatio ex nihilo* could not fill up the gap, as the *creatio ex nihilo* could not affect the principles and essences of things which, under any circumstances, must be co-eternal with God.

"God is all things in their idea, and as a whole, and in the unity of their existence: but he is not all things individually, or in their particular and fragmentary existence; he is not what the thing is, of which he is the principle. God is the thought, the idea, the essence of the universe. The thought of God, for the very reason that it, the essence, is Providence of each being particularly. The Providence of the plant is its *idea*, according to which it is born, it grows, and dies. And so it is with everything."

The eminent French eclectic, Cousin, says: "The universe itself is so far from exhausting God, that many of the attributes of God are there covered with an obscurity almost impenetrable, and are discovered only in the soul of man. *God is at once* substance and cause, at the summit of being and at its humblest degree, infinite and finite, together, triple, in fine; that is at once God, nature, and humanity. To say that the world is God is to admit only the world and deny God. However immense it may be, this world is finite, compared to God, who is infinite; and from his inexhaustible infinitude he is able to draw, without limit, new worlds, new beings, new manifestations. Invisible and present, revealed and withdrawn in himself, in the world and out of the world, communicating himself without cessation and remaining incommunicable, he is at once the living God and the God concealed."

Epes Sargent, a distinguished writer, in his "Proof Palpable of Immortality," says: —

"The conception of God as brought into relativity by an objective universe, but at the same time existing in higher and discrete degrees of being, in the highest of which he is the absolute and perfect God, is, as I have attempted to show, not inconsistent with what we know of the nature of man. It would be no irrational speculation to hold that the divine relativity to the finite may, in its expression, vary with the character of the different earths or planets fitted for intelligent beings while passing through the discipline of a material environment; that every planet with its climate and products is adapted to the state of its rational inhabitants; that what we regard as the defects or evils of Nature as manifesting herself through our planet, are merely the emblematic reflection of our own defects or evils; and so that, as the race of man improves, the earth itself will improve.

"The idea that God, as the life and intelligence of Nature, is self-circumscribed and reduced to relativity by his own 'self-denying energy,' leads to a view of the cosmos in which all the objections of Atheism are swallowed up. God is seen no longer as the provisional or constitutional monarch whose laws can rule the universe without his aid, his functions being merely honorary. At once ground and cause, *his* life becomes the fountain of *our* life, and all Nature is transfigured with divine possibilities; man, derived and dependent as he is, becomes a free co-worker with God; evil becomes a merely negative thing, having no real being or life; all imperfections become transitional, a necessary phase of good in the making; humanity, with all its selfishness, its meanness, and its arrogance, becomes ennobled when looked at from the side of its possibilities rather than its limitations and perversions, and takes on more and more the Divine Expression. We are helped to judge of mankind by its martyrs and saints rather than by its tyrants and criminals. We feel that God is not aloof from us but working in us, the very soul of this divine Nature by which we live, and without the light and life of whose sun we could not exist a moment.

"Nor let it be said that God's circumscription as the life and soul of Nature removes God in the Highest from sympathy with our weaknesses and our wants. To sympathize with us fully, to be Love and Providence, as well as Law and Wisdom, he must be implicitly the Nature he subordinates, besides a Power independent of it. It may be objected: God cannot be perfection, if, in his self-limitation as the substance of Nature, he is also imperfection; but to this it may be replied that the experience of imperfection may be essential to the very fulness of the divine perfection; that in order to be the perfect he must exist in a self-subordinated state as the imperfect also.

"Remember, moreover, that if God is a trinity, he is in that but the prototype of man, who, in each grade of his nature, is related to God in a corresponding hypostasis. The triunity of earth-body, spirit-body, and spiritual principle, is paralleled in the three-fold nature of God; and man, in each degree, and in all together, has God as his Providence, his spiritual Ideal, and his Infinite Father. The God of his childhood's trust and wonder is restored to him; the God of his prayers is an ever-present listener. If God is unyielding law, he is also maternal tenderness and love; if he is the life of our life, he is also the moral order of the universe; and Faith is thus unchecked by Science, while Reason is reconciled with Faith.

"To many profound and to many superficial thinkers, all theistic speculation is repulsive. They would say with Hooker, 'Our safest eloquence concerning Him is our silence'; or with Sir William Hamilton, 'The highest reach of human science is the scientific recognition of human ignorance.' But the heart and the intellect continue, nevertheless, to cry, 'Oh, that I knew where I might find Him!'"

Our highest conceptions of being is person, therefore God cannot in our minds be impersonal. A spiritual existence both through and above matter carries the Deity beyond the pantheistic ideas of Anaximander, without establishing, in any sense, a material supremacy or self-existent principle in physical substance. It is claimed by some that God is neither personal nor impersonal. Even this theory would not disprove freedom of action and consequent reason governing matter through specific laws of personal consciousness. In this sense He may be "super-personal." The immortality of the soul proves a personality in man, yet borrowing its individual existence from Deity.

"The secret things of God," says Sargent, "are past finding out, because, revise our conceptions of him as we may, there still remains in his nature the infinite and the unfathomable. Without irreverence and with perfect humility, therefore, may the speculative faculty exercise itself in attaining to a conception in which reason and the heart's religious aspirations may draw nearer to a union.

"Nature is an organism through which the Divine life is forever streaming, and imparting itself to all organic forms; but this organism is only a temporary objective manifestation of God, and other universes may have preceded the present. Nature is subject to change, to the limitations of space and time, and to consequent imperfection. For in his manifestations on this material plane of being, God is limited by his own 'self-denying energy,' just as a spirit is limited by divine laws on coming within the earth-sphere. Therefore the divine life, with which the whole universe throbs, is, in a manner, automatic in its developments; and Nature, though full of signs of intelligence, seems often to be acting blindly, and as if good and evil were indifferent to her,— an appearance which results from the self-imposed limitations by which the divine action is subjected to unyielding law in expressing itself through matter in these its ultimate evolutions. Thus God in Nature becomes Relative to God the Absolute, as existing in the highest of his three states.

"To attempt to authenticate this conception of God by any reference to human analogies may seem contrary to that tendency of Science which would discredit as presumptuous all such comparisons. But it is not to limit Omnipotence by any human standard, to confess to that amount of anthropomorphism which is inseparable from the conviction that man, in a certain sense, bears the image of God. 'Man,' says St. Martin, 'is a type which must have a prototype, and that prototype is God. The body of man has a necessary relation to everything visible, and his spirit is the type of everything invisible.' One may believe this without irreverence, just as he may believe that the same law which moves the universe may move an atom.

"In man we find unmistakably the phenomenon of double consciousness. Even Professor Huxley, in his Address, Aug. 25th, 1874, before the British Association at Belfast, describes a case in which two separate lives, a normal and abnormal one, seemed to be lived at intervals by the same individual; and Dr. Carpenter, though his experience does not take in many important facts now known to be true, admits the separate states of consciousness manifested so wonderfully in somnambulism.

"A corresponding truth may be at the basis of the

conception of God as a trinity in his manifestations or modes of existence; a conception of which Schelling says: 'The philosophy of mythology proves that a Trinity of Divine Potentialities is the root from which have grown the religious ideas of all nations of any importance that are known to us.'

"We may conceive of the Supreme Being, *first*, as God in first principles, the Absolute, the Incomprehensible Unity, supremely personal and conscious, because possessing all conceivable perfections in their potency and all life in its essence; the impulse of whose developments and self-limitations is an act of will; *secondly*, as God in his relations to the universe of derived spirit and mind, and self-limited according to the measure of those relations; *thirdly*, as God in ultimates, immanent or intra-mundane, and still further limited by his descent into the environments of matter and his identification with the soul of universal nature.

"Thus God, in his highest hypostasis, is the Absolute One, having within himself, in idea and in essence, all the potencies of being, whether ultimating in what we call spirit or in matter; in his intermediate hypostasis he becomes limited by relations to the world of derived spirit and mind; in his third or lowest hypostasis he is the soul, the life, and the essence of physical Nature with all her material limitations, her *seeming* inconsistencies, immoralities, and cruelties,— all which, however, are in harmony with his beneficent purposes, one of which is that of educating intelligent beings to comprehend and enjoy what he has in store for them; in harmony, too, with his own absolute independence of all evil, that being simply privation, negation, and imperfection, without which, however, man could not be a progressive being.

"If it be said that a tri-unity of being is inconceivable in God, I might reply that it is equally inconceivable in man, and yet facts and phenomena make us realize that it exists.

"'True fortitude of understanding,' says Paley, 'consists in not suffering *what we know* to be disturbed by what we do *not* know. The uncertainty of one thing does not necessarily affect the certainty of another thing. Our ignorance of many points need not suspend our assurance of a few.'

"'We should live,' says Seneca, 'as if we were living in the sight of all men; we should think as though some one could and can gaze into our inmost breast.'

"'To ask,' says the late J. W. Jackson, 'why God did not make a perfect creation is equivalent to asking that God in ultimates, on the plane of time and space, where he is to our perceptions necessarily conditioned by the sequences of duration and the limitations of extension, shall be identical with God in first principles as the eternal and infinite.'

"No anthropomorphic argument from design is needed when the Pantheistic conception is made supplementary to the Theistic. 'Analogies,' says Picton, 'which would turn our unspeakable worship of the Infinite One into the familiar admiration felt for the inventor of a new machine, are increasingly felt, in these times, to be two-edged weapons, with which

Faith does ill to play. For only by the recognition that adaptation of means to an end, in order of time, belongs to temporal and fragmentary life, not to eternal Being, do we preserve the attitude of soul which is unassailable by the bewilderments of false analogy or materialistic despair.'

"Thus we feel that we are surrounded, both on the material plane of being and on the spiritual, 'by an omnipresent, immutable Power, for whom nothing is too great, nothing too insignificant, but which equally regulates the orbits of worlds and the position of an atom, and in whose divine order there is nothing common or unclean, but its fitting place is found for the lowest as well as the highest in the palpitating life of the universe.'

"The great teacher of scientific induction, Bacon, says: 'So far are physical causes from drawing men off from God and Providence, that, on the contrary, the philosophers employed in discovering them can find no rest but by flying to God or Providence at last.'

"'The *heart* of man,' says Picton, 'recoils and always will recoil from that ghastly sense of universal death, which comes with the momentary imagination of a Godless world; but the *mind* of man is equally intolerant of obviously untenable propositions, maintained on grounds of supposed expediency.'

"'There is no resting-place for a religion of the reason,' says Mansell, 'but Pantheism or Atheism.'

"And yet, for a religion that is not of the reason, who can feel respect, and what certainty of enduring influence can be hoped for it?

"As Atheism must be reversed, and lost in that

higher Pantheism which regards the whole universe as instinct with divine life and intelligence, so must this higher Pantheism be encircled by the still higher Theism which, while it regards God as *in* Nature, regards him at the same time as *beyond* Nature, — at once the God in whom we live and move and have our being, the God of the material and spiritual universe, and the God transcendent, absolute, and infinite, the incomprehensible Unity." *

Rev. Joseph Cook says : —

"Many of the replies made to Professor Tyndall, however, miss the central point in his scheme of thought, and endeavor to show that it is madness to imagine that matter, as now and for centuries defined by Science, can evolve organization and life. But no one has proclaimed the insanity of such a supposition more vigorously than Tyndall has himself. 'These evolution notions,' he exclaims, 'are absurd, monstrous, and fit only for the intellectual gibbet, in relation to the ideas concerning matter which were drilled into us when young.' Most assuredly, Professor Tyndall does not propose 'to sweep up music with a broom,' or 'to produce a poem by the explosion of a type foundry'! Audacities of that sort are to be left to the La-Mettries and Cabanis and Holbachs; they are not attempted even by the Büchners and Carl Voigts and Moleschotts and DuBois Raymonds, who, with some whom Tyndall too much resembles, are now obsolete or obsolescent in Germany. 'If a man is a materialist,' said Professor Tholuch to me once, as we walked up and down

---

* Epes Sargent, in Palpable Proof of Immortality.

a celebrated long arbor in his garden at Halle, 'we Germans think he is not educated.' In the history of speculation so many forms of the materialistic theory have perished that a chance of life for a new form can be found in nothing less fundamental than a change in the definition of matter. Tyndall perceives, as every one must who has any eye for the signs of the times in modern research, that if Waterloos are to be fought between opposing schools of Science, or between Science and Theology or Philosophy, the majestic line of shock and onset must be this one definition. 'Either let us open our doors freely to the conception of creative acts,' he says in the sentence which best indicates his point of view in his Belfast Address, 'or, abandoning them, let us radically change our notions of matter.'

"Now, it is singular, and yet not singular, that one can find nowhere in Tyndall's writings the changed definition on which everything turns. The following four propositions, all stated in his own language, taken from different parts of his recent discussions, are the best approach to a definition that I have been able to find, in examining all he has ever published on Materialism:—

"1. Emotion, intellect, will, and all their phenomena, were once latent in a fiery cloud. I discern in matter the promise and potency of every form and quality of life. Who will set limits to the possible play of molecules in a cooling planet? Matter is essentially mystical and transcendental.

"2. Supposing that in youth we had been impregnated with the notion of the poet Goethe instead of the notion of the poet Young, looking at matter not as brute matter, but as the living garment of God, is it not probable that our repugnance to the idea of primeval union between spirit and matter might be considerably abated?

" 3. Granting the nebula and its potential life, the question, Whence come they? would still remain to baffle and bewilder us. The hypothesis does nothing more than transport the conception of life's origin to an indefinitely distant past.

" 4. Philosophical defenders of the doctrine of uniformity . . . have as little fellowship with the atheist, who says that there is no God, as with the theist, who professes to know the mind of God. ' Two things,' says Immanual Kant, ' fill me with awe, — the starry heavens and the sense of moral responsibility in man.' . . . The scientific investigator finds himself overshadowed by the same awe."

The Rev. John Weiss, with more charity than many have displayed in discussing Professor Tyndall's Address, says : —

" His subject included a sketch of the development of human thought in its effort to explain phenomena, from its first rude impulse to its latest expression in the theories of Darwin and Spencer. Nowhere else can we find so clear and thorough a statement of those theories, stripped of scientific terms, reduced to the essential points, and set in the clear light of the understanding. This alone gives value to the Address. But Professor Tyndall made the occasion one that the Germans would call epoch-making, by devoting the same clearness and coolness of statement to explain his belief in the vitality of two things, — of universal matter, and of the religious sentiment. It is plain that he has been, and is destined to be, misunderstood on these points; and as they have never been so distinctly connected before by any man of scientific pre-eminence, and as the connection involves the problem of free religion, it is worth while to take a just estimate of his thought and of its bearings upon the most important spiritual themes.

"The misunderstanding will arise, I think, chiefly in that portion of the Address which contrasts the old mechanical ideas of a lifeless matter with the new idea, which he unequivocally espouses, that matter has eternally contained all the germs of all the things which have appeared and all the forces needed to make them appear. It is material and life in combination. He says we are reduced to making a choice between two theories. One is the old one, that everything has been created out of dead matter by successive irruptions of a live Creator, in a series of creative acts. This reduces matter to a merely physical and mechanical something, not vital, but made to be a medium of vitality. He thinks that Darwin, and all the other advocates of gradual evolution, have shown that theory to be no longer tenable, by showing what minute unfoldings and gradations and modifications have taken place through enormous stretches of time, by a method of nature which never requires a special interference, and provides no points where it might occur. These facts compel him to prefer the theory that the universe is live matter, in various forms and stages of development; that it has been from all eternity alive, whether thin as gas or dense as granite; that the imagination cannot force itself back to a time when it was anything else than this, — the something containing the latent possibility of everything, the force and the germ being in the one original parcel; all forms, no matter how different they appear now to human observation, having been originally involved in this eternally live substance. A floating particle of dust, a flashing gem, a sluggish polyp, the instinct of animals and the self-consciousness of man, the savage, the sage, the prophet, the poet, were all comprised once in a homogeneous ocean, a something possible, unparticularized, but containing all particulars and all the vitality that each particular requires. Give this primitive condition of all things, in which no one thing was distinguishable, plenty of time, and all things picked themselves out, selected their forms, maintained them, transmitted the original tendency; so that here we are, because at first we were; then latent, now separated and described." *

Thus, through this wide range of quotation, including sympathizers with various sects and professions, who have with great beauty, force, and logic combated the arguments of Professor Tyndall, the great scientist gets no sympathy in any principle pointing towards Atheism.

---

*A discourse by Rev. John Weiss, preached to the 28th Congregational Society, Boston, Sept. 13, 1874.

ESSAY III.

SPIRIT AND MATTER.

"An impulse," says Professor Tyndall, "inherent in primeval man turned his thoughts and questionings betimes towards the sources of natural phenomena. The same impulse, inherited and intensified, is the spur of scientific action to-day. Determined by it, by a process of abstraction from experience, we form physical theories which lie beyond the pale of experience, but which satisfy the desire of the mind to see every natural occurrence resting upon a cause. In forming their notions of the origin of things, our earliest historic (and doubtless, we might add, our prehistoric) ancestors pursued, as far as their intelligence permitted, the same course. They also fell back upon experience, but with this difference — that the particular experiences which furnished the weft and woof of their theories were drawn, not from the study of Nature, but from what lay much closer to them — the observation of men. Their theories accordingly took an anthropomorphic form. To supersensual beings, which, ' however potent and invisible, were nothing but a species of human creatures, perhaps raised from among mankind, and retaining all human passions and appetites,'* were handed over the rule and governance of natural phenomena."

The substance of the above quotation may be partially true, but probably erroneous in the greater part of its deductions. It may prove or disprove the argument of the Professor according to the way in which it is technically rendered or understood. "An impulse" may be inherent through physical man, and yet not be material but spiritual, living beyond the decay and dissolution of the animal organism or tenement of occupation. The Deity is harmonious in his work, and never makes a human body without a soul, however small the spiritual germ may be. This impulse may have been entirely different in primeval or prehistoric man, from what we know of the condition of mankind at the present day.

This might be presupposed by the Professor, especially when we take into consideration his sympathy with the theories of Mr. Darwin, whom he quotes very extensively in his Address. The primeval man may have seen differently, thought differently, and felt differently from the man of the present day, and yet his impulse of "evolution" be from the same source as that of ours,—a spirit motor, emanating from a Deity of constituencies, and with powers entirely independent of our possible conceptions of physical matter, at the same time containing a living principle entirely distinct from it. This self-conscious, spiritual impulse, acting upon the brain of the man in all ages, has created a second power or intelligence,

---

* Hume's Natural History of Religion.

though having no consciousness separate from both a spiritual and physical union, which, to a certain extent, may be inherited and enlarged from generation to generation. The brain and intellect borrow their intelligent motive-force from spirit, which never dies, and find capacity for action and influence in the development or enlargement of every function of progressive animal life. These capacities of organization and force must have materially changed from the early days of prehistoric man down to the present time.

In reasoning from these standpoints, Mr. Darwin found difficulties which are not easily overcome, and Professor Tyndall, as yet, has not removed the obstacles. It is as difficult to find and bring forward evidence of the character of special existences in prehistoric man, whether mental, magnetic, or physical, as it is to judge accurately of the physical condition of the earth ten miles below the surface, the constituent elements of which may exist in forms equivalent to those shown in the crust upon which we dwell, but of which positive proof has always been lacking. It will be difficult to establish a molecular existence that is intelligent, though force and action may be generated, life-like, in atomic combinations. These forces, however, must ever be dissolved on the disintegration of bodies which, when aggregated, borrow impulse through laws of attraction and repulsion.

The soul and intellect of man open a way, both through intuition and reason, to physical theories and principles which lie beyond. These have a common impulse to examine and understand the phenomena of animal life, and its agencies in perpetuating, beyond their own individual possibilities, an enlarged spiritual and never-dying existence. The union of these forces is not always perfect. We have evidences around us at times that they have a distinct individual or independent existence through this apparent disjointure, sometimes the one and sometimes the other disappearing, and this so far as to leave the existence of the other doubtful. But however this may be, it is certain that the body, as a mere tenement of the spirit and mind, dies, and becomes disorganized. But Science has never yet furnished, and probably never will furnish, a particle of evidence that the life principle, or the soul, of that body died with it, though as an independent life-force, it may follow its disintegrated elements to a new organization. On the contrary, our own consciousness and sensation furnish daily and hourly proof that the spirit lives beyond the flesh, and is inherent in man through the impulses given by God alone. Historic time, it is presumed, travels but a small distance back compared to what may be called the prehistoric; and *desire*, which may be termed an inspiration of soul, mind, and the material body, reaches much further, borrowing support on its way from all evidences within its comprehension.

This impulse grasps and forms theories of that mysterious evolution which has followed man from his first appearance from the hands of his Maker, down to that present condition which to-day proves, probably stronger than ever, the existence of an independent spiritual life. The human mind naturally seeks a knowledge of the development of matter in all the forms in which it exists around us, and Science steps in to enlighten it in its researches. Barren, indeed, will that mind ever be, however, which seeks to prove, through its own dogmatisms, that the end is reached, that the laws of matter are primitive, and that spirit life, which must pre-exist before the origin of matter, is only secondary in the creation of that unfathomable universe even now but slowly opening to the mind of man. It is probably true that both the early and late inhabitants of the earth, as a whole, have, in a large sense, been students of nature. It is only the more cultivated who follow precedent. A large portion of the true development of scientific investigation, which is given us at the present day, has been through individual studies of nature, oft isolated and without the advantages of scientific books or associations. Mistakes of natural principles and their eliminations, though differing in degree according to the magnitude of such cultivation by the student who depends upon the experience of previous investigators for his basis, are oftener made, than by him who plods along alone, perhaps unaided and unsustained, till he discovers a law which he can eliminate with certainty. The reasonings and physical demonstrations of the student, acting upon texts and formulas of his professor, will often exemplify some other truth or fiction, or contradict his own hypothesis. Professor Tyndall, learned as he is, both as a student of nature and of art, with his great versatility of talent, and taste for research and demonstration, to a certain extent has fallen into the same error.

This is particularly true where he attempts to prove the independent primary character of existing life-forces in nature, which perish with the disintegration of individual bodies, thus virtually denying the existence of spirit, the life and force of all action through material combinations. He claims that the mind became early clouded by superstitious beliefs, and that the religious or anthropomorphic bias has been the great drawback of Science. Had it not been for this, if we draw the correct inference from his writings, the sky would ever have been clear for scientific investigation, and man ere this might have comprehended, not only the origin but the end of his existence, and all this through the revelations of molecular and atomic construction, — in a word, that spirit as an independent intelligent force only exists in, but dies with, the organization of the physical man.

We will not only assume, as the Professor may already have done, that the molecule is the primary source of the atom, and creates it, through its own dissolution, but go beyond anything we have yet heard suggested from scientists, and fix a character for both that would much help the Professor's theory, without injuring our own. This, of course, we do somewhat at the risk of weakening the hypothesis we set up; but the exposition is fearless, nevertheless, and is one that, by all means, should be understood. If materialists can make anything from it inconsistent with the existence of "spirit" as an independent principle from matter, they are welcome to do so.

What are Molecules and Atoms; what is their size, condition, and essence; what relation do they bear to each other; and what their life-force and mechanical action? *

Professor Tyndall has not explained this to the common mind, if he has to his peers. The popular mind is ready to receive and recognize any principle in physics bearing upon mechanical questions within its compass, and give them life and motion, either through material or spiritual energies, as the case may be; such minds only require that tangibility shall find place in their code of application to the industrial arts. We would then venture to clothe molecules and atoms with all the temporary vitality, essence, and conditions attributed or accorded to them by Professor Tyndall, though still lacking *independent* life energies.

Passing down the formula of creative existences from Deity, through Will; Force, Motion; Spirit, Soul; Action, Ether; Electricity, Magnetism,—we come to Molecules and Atoms. We believe molecules may be divided into two classes, ponderable and imponderable,—the former in a sense representing the constituents of "atoms," or porous and solid physical matter; while the latter may be called the integral or representative of the more subtile and pungent life-like forces, as Action, Ether, Electricity, Magnetism, the Gases, etc. Ponderable molecules may also be hollow, but ever represent two forces, a positive and negative: to the positive is due expan-

---

* See Plate 2.

sion and contraction, under force and motion; to the negative, which may be said to form a coating or shell around the positive, resistance.

Molecule, then, is the parent or source of Atom, which is the slag produced and thrown off from molecular action and decomposition. While the ponderable Molecule is a result of the workings of the two great first physical principles in nature * (next to spirit), and consequently contains a life principle more pungent and subtile than any yet recognized by scientists, Atoms, either singly or in the aggregate form, independent of gravity, possess only the powers of attraction and repulsion, and these when acted upon by other forces.

Molecules, on the contrary, are independently active at all times as against any principle not anterior to their own existence. In these forces we recognize an action kindred with the principles of physical and animal life, not intelligence, mind, or spirit, the latter of which only comes from Deity, and the former a result of the combination of spirit with animal life. The forms, sources, and action of molecules, ponderable or imponderable, may be various, however infinitesimal in size, but as yet have not been measured.

The two primary physical principles used in the construction of the whole universe, which we have called Action and Ether, as positive and negative energies, are, after the first impulse of Divine will, always active, and may continue so till that will is withdrawn.

---

* Action and Ether.

No doubt these, as individual antagonistic active forces, generating both ponderable and imponderable molecules, are constantly changing conditions or destroying each other. This process may be considered the working of unconscious life-forces, that are the nearest approach to the conscious. The result of this effort is material substance emanating from consuming molecules forming corpuscles and "atoms," which aggregate in various forms, and take their place in the active field of matter under laws of Physics. Even though going further than Professor Tyndall in furnishing two independent physical principles primary to the mechanical construction of a molecule, that, according to his theory, might be endowed with perpetual motion, we do not claim so much for it, but are willing it should borrow, with all other physical matter, its life from the will of Deity.

If the illustration of the Molecule and Atom should stop here, it is possible they might not be considered perfectly clear to every mind, even to one that has some definite idea of both as already described; but when further considered, and coupled with the illustration of the workings of light, heat, cold, human blood, color, ice, water, steam, and other elements, it will be found that an individual secondary force and creative power is given to molecules, far beyond that in any description delineated by Professor Tyndall, without even the most distant claim of a life-force independent of the essence or prerogatives of Infinity. An apple falls from a tree in obedience to a law: it will not be claimed that that law comprehends intelligence, but only force. The impulse of gravity will be governed by the amount and density of the mass, not by its intelligence. The aggregation and bulk of matter or atoms will thus accelerate or retard the motion. A worm or beetle, both possessing intelligence, will fall as quick as a pebble of the same size and weight, unless the intelligence of the former is used in resistance to its downward force.

Motion, as a principle, is not life, but a condition. Intelligence must possess life,— therefore uniting two principles in one action. Consciousness must exist beyond matter, as intelligence through inspiration passes from and beyond the source of material being, to an independent existence afar off, through a mental instead of a physical volition. Important truths have been known to travel many miles without the aid of the least physical conductor, and entirely through a spiritual or mental projective force. This force may have started from, and been received by, a physical body; but in the space of transmission it could not have belonged to either.

Professor Tyndall thinks the more penetrating intellects of our race are among the least satisfied with what is equivalent to a religious faith; and in ancient times this class of minds soon tried to connect natural phenomena with their physical principles. This we think is an error, as history furnishes a large class of the most eminent men of nearly every age, who were in some sense religious devotees. He thinks the Sciences were born under the influences of the commercial aristocracy of Greece, in connection with their Eastern neighbors. He mingles the gods of heathen mythology with the Christian's God in the denunciations of Euripides and others, where there was declared a "determination to sweep from the field of theory this mob of gods and demons, and to place natural phenomena as a basis more congruent with themselves." "Atoms and Molecules" thus were to become the force and material of construction, and an independent world of matter, life, and action was to be evolved.

THE NEW YORK
PUBLIC LIBRARY

ASTOR, LENOX AND
TILDEN FOUNDATIONS

Spiral
Nebula

ESSAY IV.

MATERIAL LIFE-FORCES.

"WITH regard to the influence," says Professor Tyndall, " wielded by Aristotle in the Middle Ages, and which, though to a less extent, he still wields, I would ask permission to make one remark. When the human mind has achieved greatness and given evidence of extraordinary power in any domain, there is a tendency to credit it with similar power in all other domains. Thus theologians have found comfort and assurance in the thought that Newton dealt with the question of revelation, forgetful of the fact that the very devotion of his powers, through all the best years of his life, to a totally different class of ideas, not to speak of any natural disqualification, tended to render him less instead of more competent to deal with theological and historical questions. Goethe, starting from his established greatness as a poet, and indeed from his positive discoveries in Natural History, produced a profound impression among the painters of Germany when he published his 'Farbenlehre,' in which he endeavored to overthrow Newton's theory of colors. This theory he deemed so obviously absurd that he considered its author a charlatan, and attacked him with a corresponding vehemence of language. In the domain of Natural History Goethe had made really considerable discoveries; and we have high authority for assuming that, had he devoted himself wholly to that side of science, he might have reached in it an eminence comparable with that which he attained as a poet. In sharpness of observation, in the detection of analogies, however apparently remote, in the classification and organization of facts according to the analogies discerned, Goethe possessed extraordinary powers. These elements of scientific inquiry fall in with the discipline of the poet; but on the other hand, a mind thus richly endowed in the direction of Natural History may be almost shorn of endowment as regards the more strictly-called physical and mechanical sciences. Goethe was in this condition. He could not formulate distinct mechanical conceptions; he could not see the force of mechanical reasoning; and in regions where such reasoning reigns supreme he became a mere *ignis fatuus* to those who followed him."

Sir Isaac Newton lived and died a Christian, and left a record in Science and Philosophy which few have equalled, or will ever be able to eclipse. Goethe's pretensions may have been less than the future interpretations of his vast literary labors may warrant. Time opens much in the history of a great mind that may not be revealed through his writings in his day and generation. It will be clear to every reader of Goethe's history, that whatever his honors or distinctions above his associates, his mind was never clouded by man-worship to that degree that he could not see and feel the influence of a Deity ever round and about him, nor did he deny a spirit existence beyond the grave. Of that part of his work dedicated to colors, we cannot properly judge from the mistaken standpoint from which he viewed what had been termed, but what was not, Newton's theory of light. It is perhaps difficult at this time to account for the erroneous definition of Newton's theory, which has led the world so long astray. Goethe was mistaken, as many others have been; otherwise his theory of colors might never have been written. He, like thousands of others, took the ordinary encyclopedial idea that Newton believed and taught that "light was composed of colors," which Newton in his "Interpretations" distinctly denies. The theory always attributed to Sir Isaac, that *white light* is made of colors, is so prevalent that teachers often encourage students in the vain attempts to produce pure white from variously colored pigments by mixture, — a theory as impossible as for the eye not to distinguish any but white rays in the colors of the rainbow or in the flashes of the aurora borealis. If Goethe became a "a mere *ignis fatuus* to those who followed him," he certainly was not then, nor would he now be, in that respect, alone in his attempts to enlighten the world through scientific teachings.* The scientist for centuries has assumed that the earth supply of light, as light, and heat, as heat, flows wholly from the sun, while all evidence we can get on that subject proves that the nearer we approach the sun from the surface of the earth, the darker and colder we find it; that this great volume of heat and light that we

---

* See Plate I.

enjoy, so small in comparison to what scientists estimate the whole volume of the heat of the sun to be, is generated on the surface of the sun, and is precipitated against the force of gravity, by undulation through space, to and through our atmosphere, which of itself is so cold, only seven miles from the earth's surface, as to paralyze any one ascending to that height. Is not the Action theory,* which provides the emission of a subtile fluid from the sun towards his planets, but which is not necessarily "light" or "heat" till it reaches the atmosphere, through undulation, producing both by combustion with it, as consistent a theory for the earth's supply? Without irreverence, would it not be at least more economical? Would not Mercury be more consistently habitable than now, under the old theory, which would make her substance so much hotter than molten iron? Would not Neptune seem a little more like what the great Creator would build up for mankind, if it had, as all the intermediate planets may have, an equable light and heat, through the consumption of Action and Ether thus supplied? At present, under the old theory, its degree of cold must be as much more intense than that producing ice as is the heat enveloping Mercury more than that we enjoy on the surface of our earth. In the light and heat from the gas we burn we detect no difference, whether the pipe containing it is one or five miles from the fountain of supply. May we not thus infer the supply of light and heat for the solar system, or must we, through claims to Science, attribute to Deity

---

* See Plate II.

absolute absurdities at times, when reasoning from cause and effect, as old theories compel us to do?

Professor Proctor, in his Astronomical Lectures, says:—

"One hundred and eight times does the sun's diameter exceed that of the earth, and the surface of the sun exceeds that of the earth 108 times 108 times, or 11,600 times, while the volume of the sun exceeds that of the earth 1,250,000 times. But the mass of the sun is not so much greater than the earth. It would appear as though the body of the sun were constituted of matter about a quarter lighter on an average than that which constitutes the earth, and the result is that the sun's mass, instead of exceeding the mass of the earth 1,250,000 times, only exceeds it 315,000 times.

"But now," continues Professor Proctor, "let us pass from the question of the sun's might, to its heat and light.

"The sun is the source of all these forms of light and life which exist upon the earth. That is no idle dream. Every form of force upon the earth, every action that we perform, all the forms of energy we know of, even the very thoughts we think, may be said to come from the sun. It is by the sun's heat that life is maintained upon the earth.

"And now, as to the quantity of that heat. Sir John Herschel, in the south of Africa, made experiments to determine the actual quantity of heat that is received from the sun. The heat there was so great that at the depth of four inches below the sand the thermometer rose to 160°. He was able to cook a steak by placing it in a box covered with glass, and that inside another box with a glass cover, and to boil eggs hard. He made experiments, and found in the first place, that about one fourth of the sun's light and heat was cut off at midday by the air; and taking that into account, and making the requisite calculation for a large extent of surface, he found that the quantity of the sun's heat that fell on an area of one square mile would be sufficient to melt, in a single hour, 26,000 tons of ice. Well, now that is merely the quantity received by a square mile of the earth's surface. But the earth presents to the sun a surface (regarding her for a moment as a flat disk) 50,000,000 square miles in extent. And then how small is the quantity of the sun's light and heat that this earth actually captures. You have only to consider how small the sun looks in the heavens, and consider how small our earth would look beside him, with this small diameter compared with his, of one inch to three yards, and you can see how small a proportion of the sun's heat we capture. By a calculation which can be readily made, it is found that only the 2,000.000,000th part, or less than that proportion of the sun's heat, is captured by the earth; and all the planets together receive only one 227,000,000th part of the sun's heat. Here is another mystery the study of Astronomy presents: only one part in 227,000,000 parts appears to be applied to any useful purpose, and the rest seems wasted. It is not for us to judge of the operations of Nature. But here, at any rate, do we seem to find a confirmation of the saying of the atheist that sounds so strange to us, that 'Nature, in

MATERIAL LIFE-FORCES. 65

filling a wine-glass, upsets a gallon.' There is the sun's heat being continually sent forth, and only the 227,000,000th part received. Only imagine a merchant who spent large sums of money, and who employed only one cent usefully for every, $2000,000 of his income! And that is what the sun appears to be continually doing. The actual emission of solar light and heat corresponds to what would be obtained if on every square yard of the sun's surface, six tons of coal were consumed every hour. In every second, the sun gives out as much heat as would be given out by burning 11,600,000,000,000,000 tons."

Professor Tyndall calls Heat "a mode of motion." So must be Cold. Either will produce an electric current, positive or negative as the case may be, not necessarily carrying heat or cold with it. This may be true of both, without either being the origin of motion. Motion may be the origin of Heat and Cold, as they are conditions merely, and their action, simple expansion and contraction; while imponderable molecular force may be the life or cause of action in whatever degree it may be observable, actienic and etheric impact furnishing the energy.

Animal blood may be supposed to form an exception to all fluid matter, in the fact that a trinity of forces are constantly at work in its sustenance.* The molecular action of this fluid must be through ponderable and imponderable energies, with distinctive electric and magnetic co-operators. All these principles are ever active in the blood, and through them circulation and distribution is provided by expansion and

---
* See Plate II.

contraction of molecules, and magnetic attraction. Blood, of all material substances, approaches the nearest to independent animal life, and yet, when spirit is separated, how soon it dies.

Color is a condition created by light and shade, and in air or fluids its magnitude or hue is generally governed by the angle from which the light of observation is cast.

We can judge but little of color beyond our atmosphere. The rays of actienic light reaching us from above will always be colored differently to our view, according to the density, rarity, and humidity of the belt that, for the time being, is stratified over our heads. A ray of light flowing in a straight line, with no intervening obstacle, will ever be white to our vision. When it is thrown from a straight line, from any cause, whether it be by prism, cloud, or vapor, it overlaps other rays, creating shades, varying as they may be intercepted by light from other directions, and the thickness of the plates, the colors produced being governed by the angle of reflection or refraction, as the case may be. The spectroscope often, if not always, plays false by breaking the regular waves of undulation, and creating different colors in the surrounding atmosphere, instead of transmitting, as is supposed, the true color belonging to foreign substances.

Ice, water, vapor, and steam may be traced back to molecules, the various conditions being chargeable to the occasional conditions to which they are subjected.*

Ice will emit vapor when the surrounding atmos-

---
* See Plate II.

phere is below the freezing point. This vapor rises against the laws of gravity. A general vaprous expansion does not meet the case, so far as to enable the humid matter to rise through an atmosphere more than seven hundred times lighter. Individual molecular expansion would only account for it, even independent of attraction. Under the actinic combustion necessary to disintegrate a molecule of water from ice, the hydrogen gas may, in some form, create for itself a shell of oxygen, if mechanically combined, making each individual molecule a simple balloon for the time being, which would take it up as generated. Vapor in the atmosphere must of necessity be so diffused as to be permeated with the molecules of common air, destroying the old theory of its general buoyancy, which can only be reasonably accounted for from the real nature of its specific individual molecular character. A molecule of steam is a simple bubble; it may be filled with hydrogen or other gas or heated air. The former would account for its suspension for a long time in clouds above us; the latter for a quick condensation with rain or snow. Thus we can theorize life-forces far beyond, and much more consistent than, those of the atoms of Democritus, which of themselves were dead. Our atoms are also inanimate physical matter, but our molecules have life, pungency, force, and we have to acknowledge for them a spirit motor beyond.

Thus, through the lighting of our houses with gas drawn from a reservoir afar off, the common mind borrows an idea of infinity in lighting the heavens; while by heating our dwellings with furnace-coal, hundreds of miles from the quarry, we accomplish a practical fact, — not possible by its consumption in or near its original bed. A beneficent Creator goes beyond our possible conceptions, and gives us both light and heat through the consumption of two simple original principles in nature.

Rev. Mr. Weiss, in the sermon before referred to, asked Professor Tyndall this question: —

"How do you get your eternally live matter started? And that question will always be in order so long as the human mind is so built that it must inquire for causes. One of the elements of vitality in this live matter must have been this pertinacity for tracing things to their sources, for tracing its own mother, then live matter, to its source. How can we escape from this? There was, we will suppose, an eternally vital matter. Was vitality materialized, or was matter vitalized? That is to say, can the human mind conceive of any mode of existence previous to this simultaneous life and matter?"

If this question can be answered in any other form than that the "live matter" must be set in motion by its author, we know not the secret, and must plead ignorance of the way and means.

Mr. Weiss further adds: —

"Now, if being unwilling, for moral reasons, to be pantheistic, we reply that there must have been a something previous, a pure, bodiless, matterless spirit, we avoid Pantheism only verbally; we put up a use of language to suppose what the mind cannot conceive. We cannot conceive of a fulness of spirit that depended upon being utterly bereft and void of matter. That is 'a dream of the shadow of smoke.' It is a so-called spiritual view set up to pick a personal Deity out of an eternal universe. . . .

"If any material became evolved, it must have been latent in the life-force or spirit. For spirit that was not always holding material in solution could not have taken a single step towards contriving material and maintaining vital relations with it.

"But Professor Tyndall appears to explain his live matter in such a manner as to dispense altogether with all creative acts. He does not intend to state it in this way, but he will be misunderstood to do it in his scientific eagerness to reach simplicity of treatment by avoiding all language that has taken airs from having been much with theology. He says he cannot put his finger on a spot where creative interference was required. But what is his gradual method of nature but gradual creative continuance?"

Professor Tyndall thinks that "Science demands the radical extirpation of caprice," yet it is doubtful whether there is a class of educated people who are more capricious than Materialists. He thinks that Bacon's estimate of Democritus would place the latter above Plato or Aristotle, "though their philosophy was noised and celebrated in the schools, amid the din and pomp of professors." Without undertaking to decide between the three contestants, it may be pertinent to ask Professor Tyndall whether the present age is any exception to the habit of *mutual laudation* of professors, even if not done "amid din and pomp." He thinks "Genseric, Attila, and the barbarians destroyed the Atomic Philosophy." If this was the fact, the disaster could not certainly be laid, as he claims, to religionists, whether they were superstitious or otherwise.

"Lange," says Tyndall, "considers the relation of Epicurus to the gods subjective,— the indication probably of an ethical requirement of his own nature. We cannot read history with open eyes, or study human nature to its depths, and fail to discern such a requirement. Man never has been, and he never will be, satisfied with the operations and products of the understanding alone; hence, Physical Science cannot cover all the demands of his nature. But the history of the efforts made to satisfy these demands might be broadly described as a history of errors, the error, in great part, consisting in ascribing fixity to that which is fluent, which varies as we vary, being gross when we are gross, and becoming, as our capacities widen, more abstract and sublime."

Has there any principle been less fixed for the last two thousand years than the scientific principle as taught by any class of scientists existing within that period?

Professor Tyndall describes Aristotle and his followers as being void of *imagination*, which he properly thinks necessary for physical conceptions, though he does not like the associations of the word. In this respect he quotes Pascal as being more clear and vivid in description. If Professor Tyndall would substitute *impressibility* for *imagination*, he would recognize a condition in the human mind nearer fitted to a warm and clear appreciation of both Religion and Science than Aristotle possessed.

"There is in imagination," says Buckle, "a divine and prophetic power, and an insight into things which, if properly used, would make it the ally of Science instead of the enemy. By the poet, nature is contemplated on the side of the emotions; by the man of science, on the side of understanding: they are as truthful; they are as likely to be right. They obey fixed laws; they follow an orderly and uniform course; they run in sequences; they have their logic and method of inference. Poetry, therefore, is a part of Philosophy, simply because the emotions are a part of the mind. If the man of science despises their teaching, so much the worse for him."

"Professor Tyndall," says Mr. Weiss, "cannot ignore the main point, though his language seems to swerve from it, viz. How did matter become vitalized by this magnificent method which we call natural selection? We see that there has been a slow accumulation of results, that grow more complex, but at the same time more definite, till they attain to permanence. But how did Nature start with this drift to accumulate objects in this way, and to self-register herself? There has been some fashioning drift slowly struggling through Nature's principle of selection, and all things have been spontaneously done. But, I ask, whence comes Nature's power to do all things in this spontaneous way, without the intervention of the old-fashioned Creator?"

"But Professor Tyndall prefers to think that all these apparent marks of design illustrate the method of Nature, 'and not the technic of a man-like artificer.' Instead of supposing that a Deity works and adapts and modifies, plots and reflects, as a man does, to reach certain results, he supposes that each result is a natural resultant of a whole neighborhood of results, and that the adaptation of one thing to another came to pass through stages of perfection by the addition of 'increment to increment of infinitesimal change,' so that 'the exquisite climax of the whole' is a result of natural selection. And here again it is plain that a finer idea of the creative method solicits our admiration. It is a much more subtile process, held by nicer links and a more even logic, when all the objects of nature gradually make their own environment, take what benefit can be derived from it, and let the benefit react upon the environment till insensibly another modification of it is reached, and other objects, than if a Creator should make a number of objects with the design of accommodating them to each other by subsequent contrivances. In the former process the objects are not invented on purpose to show what fine contrivances can be introduced to make them mutually convenient; for there never was a moment in the whole eternity of them when they were not mutually convenient; when, in fact, nature let no objects survive that were not mutually adaptive. All the rest died out because they could not be adapted; the force and matter that was on the spot could make nothing of them; the environment left them not a peg to hang from; if a personal Creator had intervened he could have contrived nothing to rescue them from the minute difference which gave an advantage to the survivors, and saved them to become adapted."

MATERIAL LIFE-FORCES. 73

"We have no hesitation in saying," quoting from the writings of John Weatherbee, "that the most melancholy shadow that could be thrown over, or into, the thought of the world would be the general or universal conviction that this is all of life; that when a man dies that is the end of him. Referring to Buckle again, whose thought goes below the surface into the sub-soil of human nature, he says, 'If the belief in immortality was eradicated from the human mind, it would drive most of us to despair.'

"In the mean time and now, may it not be possible that there are more than five senses? that the ray of mental light may overlap the normal mind of man, and that in happy moments some may grasp a wider spectrum of the mental ray? and that even now it may be the twilight of a more extended vision just rolling in upon the world of thought; and for some inscrutable reason, as of yore, it is hidden from the wise and prudent and revealed unto babes."

"Professor Tyndall," says the "London Spectator," "recently lectured at Manchester on 'Crystalline and Molecular Force,' and took the opportunity of some concluding remarks to distinguish his religious Agnosticism from Atheism: 'He had, not sometimes, but often in the spring-time, watched the advance of the sprouting leaves, and of the grass, and of the flowers, and observed the general joy of opening life in nature, and he had asked himself this question: Could it be that there was no being or thing in nature that knew more about these things than he did? did he in his ignorance represent the highest knowledge of these things existing in this universe? The man who put that question fairly to himself, if he was not a shallow man, if he was a man capable of being penetrated by profound thought, would never answer the question by professing that creed of Atheism which had been so lightly attributed to him.' That is, Professor Tyndall, as we understand him, has often been filled with doubts, *not* of his own thesis, that molecules and molecular forces are the ultimate seed-vessels of human life, mind, and thought, but as to whether those seed-vessels themselves did not owe their origin to a Being who understands and shapes their powers of growth.' Well, that is all perfectly consistent with what he said at Belfast. But is Professor Tyndall's peroration perfectly consistent either with that or with any other recent profession of Professor Tyndall's? ' He was afraid that many of the fears which are now entertained on these subjects really had their roots in a kind of scepticism. . . . He would exhort such men to cast out scepticism, for this fear had its root in scepticism.' We confess we don't know what the sentiment of that passage is, if it be not a delicate and refined kind of buncombe. Agnosticism *is* scepticism. If Professor Tyndall has his moments of hope that the universe if directed by a Mind, after all, but thinks it a perfectly open question, what can he mean by denouncing scepticism as a state of mind to be 'cast out'? Is there any weakness or cowardice in supposing that the universe, if it were *not* under divine government, would ultimately come to grief?"

ESSAY V.

MECHANICAL EVOLUTION.

Democritus, in his aggregation of physical substance, went as far as Atoms for a primary principle, but acknowledged that individually they did not possess sensation, and it was only in their combination that the phenomena of life arises, or that atoms of themselves contained even the principles of animal or vegetable mobility. This was going about as far as have some modern philosophers in the establishment of perpetual motion.

They have constructed a piece of mechanism that would almost move of itself, but not quite. It needed an "impulse" beyond itself. Professor Tyndall and his *confrères* have gone further than Democritus, and have furnished him a principle of action and motion in molecules.

We have endeavored to show the mechanical construction of a molecule, and where it borrows its force; but to supply that force we go back to two other principles in nature, the one positive, the other negative, to create and give life and action to the molecules. At the same time we show that even they, so far removed from atoms in all that would constitute an original life and force, and infinitely superior to them, would not of themselves move except under the influence of "spirit," the essence of God himself.

We claim that spirit, under the will of Deity, is the primary author of all conscious life and motion, and that the two next principles are physical, and are the instruments or elements used in enlarging and perpetuating the same, through the organization of mind and unconscious life-like matter, in all conditions; and that these primary energies are endowed with all the properties of continuous secondary forces through all evolution, combination, or agglomeration known in animal or physical matter.

"The principles enunciated by Democritus," says Tyndall, "reveal his uncompromising antagonism to those who deduced the phenomena of nature from the caprices of the gods."

"That great enigma, 'the exquisite adaptation of one part of an organism to another part, and to the conditions of life,' more especially the construction of the human body, Democritus made no attempt to solve. Empedocles, a man of more fiery and poetic nature, introduced the notion of love and hate among the atoms to account for their combination and separation. Noticing this gap in the doctrine of Democritus, he struck in with the penetrating thought, linked, however, with some wild speculation, that it lay in the very nature of those combinations which were suited to their ends (in other words, in harmony with their environment) to maintain themselves, while unfit combination, having no proper habitat, must rapidly disappear. Thus more than two thousand years ago the doctrine of the 'survival of the fittest,' which in our day, not on the basis of vague conjecture, but of positive knowledge, has been raised to such extraordinary significance, had received at all events partial enunciation."*

Democritus had all the advantages of wealth and extended power and influence to secure the best education of his time, and his great thirst for knowledge led him studiously to improve the opportunity. But his mind was a negative one, which, like that of his great admirer Bacon, the metaphysical and material philosopher of later times, did not easily soar above the consciousness, impulses, and appetites engendered through ambitious desires for the gratification of the senses. Bacon has been called a peculator and sycophant; while Democritus was at least a spendthrift and willing dependant on his family, after running through his own liberal patrimony. His early boyhood, as history informs us, was divided between the study of theology and astronomy under the instruction of Chaldean tutors, — two studies which Professor Tyndall, in this day, would probably not think well adapted to develop a mind of tender age. Leucippus is said to have taught him his system of atoms and of vacuum. He travelled into many parts of the world, where he found learned men, visited the priests of Egypt, from whom he studied geometry, and continued his travels to Persia, India, and Ethiopia for conference with the Gymnasophists. On his return, his general knowledge gave him position, and his negative mind and arrogance commanded tribute from the

---

*Lange.

ignorant and superstitious. He became a magistrate of distinction, but was most fond of the administration of laws of his own making. He treated life as a farce; in this, as well as in natural mirthfulness, he was unlike Bacon; but on the whole, though believing in a God and the immortality of the soul, he did not possess those qualities which would establish his character as a guide to posterity, and he made few happy during his life. The age in which he lived was one of superstition and thirst for power, and his teachings were not suited to enlighten the darkness of the one, or allay or satisfy the selfishness of the other, considered either in a religious, scientific, or philosophical sense. He died a recluse at an advanced age, — mentally, if not physically, blind.

We cannot see how Professor Tyndall supports or even improves his argument by bringing forward the name of Epicurus, who, though a student of Democritus, and to a certain extent adopting his philosophy, was different from him in every respect. The former was a poor boy, and a modest and retiring student; while the latter was rich and arrogant, and all through life showed the characteristics of a pampered mind. Epicurus had the reputation of living a "pure and serene life, and died a peaceful death." The first principles of his philosophy as laid down were atoms, space, and gravity; but he did not deny the existence of Spirit, or God, though he thought it beneath the dignity of Deity to concern himself about human affairs. This certainly shows a modesty and self-abasement not manifested in the character of Democritus. He held him, nevertheless, to use the words of an ancient writer, as a blessed, immortal being. Dispute arose early about the materiality or mentality of his theories of life, and two sects sprang up, the one claiming spiritual and the other material precedence in the pleasures recommended by the founder of the theory. Gassendi held that the " pleasure in which this philosopher has fixed the sovereign good " was nothing else but the highest tranquillity of mind in conjunction with the most perfect health of body, but others disagreed with him. One main object of Epicurus, according to Tyndall, was to free the world from superstition and the fear of death. " He adored the gods," says Tyndall, " but in the ordinary fashion." " The idea of divine power, properly purified, he thought an elevating one." In recognizing the divine Author, he lifted himself above the gods of heathen mythology, and thus only could satisfy " the special requirements of his own nature." " On one great point the mind of Epicurus was at peace : he neither sought nor expected here, or hereafter, any personal profit from his relation to the gods." This is a sublime thought, and would antedate, in its reach and principle, not only the teachings, but the death and atonement, of Christ.

Lucretius claims that the "mechanical shock of atoms " is the " all-sufficient cause of things," without defining the cause of the shock, the origin of the force, or the necessary momentum to accomplish its object in any given direction. " He also," says Professor Tyndall, " combats the notion that the constitution of nature has been in any way determined by intelligent design. The interaction of the atoms throughout infinite time rendered all manner of combinations possible." This is heresy against common-sense, for he further says, "The fit ones persisted, while the unfit ones disappeared." Not after deliberation did the atoms station themselves in the right place, nor did they bargain which motions they should assume. The first proposition of Democritus is, "From nothing comes nothing. Nothing that exists can be destroyed"; and the second, "Nothing happens by chance." How does the Professor reconcile these contradictions? He makes the shock accidental, the formation without design, and withdraws the atoms not useful in the structure. What determines the "fit ones," what principle of "accident" could select and reject, and where do the unfit ones disappear to, when "nothing that exists can be destroyed"? His grand conception of the atoms falling silently through immeasurable ranges of space and time suggested the nebulous hypothesis to Kant, its first propounder. Atoms are supposed to be ponderable, physical matter, yielding to the laws of gravity, and obeying the laws of attraction and repulsion. What more natural, under these laws, than that matter should attract matter, and aggregate it when floating in an unresisting medium; or that such should become changed at every step of progression from the highest to the lowest condition of molecular effort under known physical laws, without disputing the spirit force beyond, or claiming that the former were primary and all-sufficient of themselves?

The creation, by both divine and human revelations, must have had a beginning, and the laws of nature a system in their work. If we are able to discover the true workings of these laws in any one particular, our insight and comprehension of the rest enlarge.

Imagination and ideality have their part to play, and may first aid to compass and measure them; but intellectual research must establish and perfect them. We can build up a system, primarily, through our ideality, and may afterwards prove the same by reasoning and experiment. If we make mistakes in parts, or the whole, persevering research comes to our aid, and generally rewards us in finally arriving at the truth.

What we see of growth on our own earth convinces us of the possibility and even the facility of creating solid matter from volatile substances. The formation of the crystal on the top of high mountains, where there can be no influences other than magnetism below, and electricity in the atmosphere, and its constituents above, proves to us that a solid may be formed from fluids. Metals are dissolved and again precipitated with ease under favoring circumstancs. The action of action upon ether, as a positive against a negative force in space, would not seem mysteriously improbable as compared with other changes in nature with which we are familiar. A product must result differing from the conflicting forces, and this may be in many forms. A solid or semi-solid may result, instead of volatile substances, endowed with other generative and alterative principles. Solid nebulous matter may be formed, immediately about and around which the more volatile properties may cling, creating other changes from the nature of their own powers, and which may be augmented from other accumulating actionic and etheric decompositions taking place. But all these transformations will not account for, or prove, a life principle within themselves; the intelligence must come from beyond, — the great resource of matter, which is spirit.

"Materialism," says Sargent, "would still be confronted by the same problem, even if it were to discover a law that would explain the universe. For the law itself and the law-maker would have to be explained in their turn. Natural evolution through periods of time not to be reckoned requires an intelligent Force to account for it, just as much as would an instantaneous act of creation. The argument from design, based on analogies with the works of human artificers, is not needed. We must learn to look for divine perfection, not in the particular and fragmentary things of time, but in the universals of eternity; since here, conditioned as we are, there can be, in the very nature of things, no light without darkness, no good without evil, no truth without error, no progress without imperfection. The wise man says, 'Trust and wait.' The man not wise says, 'Since I can see no sign that God has acted as I would have acted in his place, there can be no God!'

"We have seen that spiritual and all other facts of Science are tending to resolve our conception of matter into that of force. Even Professor Huxley admits thus much. He says: 'Undoubtedly, active force is inconceivable, except as a state of consciousness, . . . except as something comparable to volition.'

"The domain of Science is bounded by the region of second causes; and therefore the idea of a First Cause, of God, can never be scientifically excluded or repressed. 'If,' says Professor Le Comte, 'in tracing the chain of causes upward, we stop at any cause or force or principle, that force or principle becomes for us God, since it is an efficient agent controlling the universe.'

"In order to be something more than mere Scepticism, and to offer a consistent theory of the universe, Atheism must abandon its negative form for a positive; and it cannot do this except by merging itself in the materialistic theory.

"We assume that something or other unmade and without beginning has existed from all eternity; for whatever exists must have its sufficient cause, either in itself or out of itself, since nothing can come from nothing, whatever Scepticism may say to the contrary.

"This self-existent something, is it unorganized matter, or is it undirected force, or is it a combination of the two?"

ESSAY VI.

TRUTH AND SOPHISTRY.

According to Prof. Tyndall, the sophists of Athens " did their work," and " ran through their career." Nowadays we have the same class, who not only are trying to do their own work, but are attempting to furnish work and principles for others. These are generally materialists and metaphysicians, selfish, cold, and dogmatic, who always claim to be the aristocracy of Science, but whom, be it said to his lasting credit, Prof. Tyndall has done much to humble.

While overthrowing many of their structures, however, he has used some of the old material as his own, which he will probably find will be the first to decay, and thus imperil the new, that otherwise might be enduring. " Whewell," says Tyndall, " makes many wise and brave remarks regarding the spirit of the Middle Ages. It was a menial spirit. The seekers after natural knowledge had forsaken that fountain of living waters, the direct appeal to nature by observation and experiment, and had given themselves up to the remanipulation of the notions of their predecessors. It was a time when thought had become abject, and when the acceptance of mere authority led, as it always does in Science, to intellectual death.

Natural events, instead of being traced to physical, were referred to moral causes, while an exercise of the fantasy, almost as degrading as the Spiritualism of the present day, took the place of scientific speculation. Then came the mysticism of the Middle Ages, — Magic, Alchemy, the Neo-Platonic Philosophy, with its visionary though sublime abstractions, which caused men to look with shame upon their own bodies as hinderances to the absorption of the creature in the blessedness of the Creator.

"Finally came the Scholastic Philosopy, a fusion, according to Lange, of the least mature notions of Aristotle with the Christianity of the West. Intellectual immobility was the result. As a traveller without a compass in a fog may wander long, imagining he is making way, and find himself, after hours of toil, at his starting-point; so the schoolmen, having tied and untied the same knots, and formed and dissipated the same clouds, found themselves, at the end of centuries, in their old position."

The Sophists had the reputation of pursuing Philosophy more for gain than for the love of truth itself, but no such charge can be made against Professor Tyndall. Like Pythagoras, he declined to take their name, and does not sympathize with their principles. From the fact that Pythagoras' own sentiments and principles were so high, it is presumed that the Sophists must have belonged to an entirely different class in mind and principle. "Pythagoras instituted," says Thirlwald, "a philosophical school, a religious brotherhood, and a political association, which was composed of young men of the noblest families, not exceeding three hundred in number." This would at least indicate that he had a religious principle, and was not an atheist; for he believed that the soul was immortal, and that the highest aim and blessedness of man is likeness to Deity. Socrates, Plato, and Aristotle, Euclid, Archimedes, and Hipparchus, each in turn accomplished a work for ancient Greece, the results of which are very much felt by the whole civilized world of the present day. This long line of philosophers, to whom the world owes so much, cannot in any sense be classed as infidels or atheists, for they taught principles of morals, religion, immortality of the soul, and belief in Deity, and did much to clear away the clouds of Materialism which at times overhung Greece and Rome. Professor Tyndall says, "The science of ancient Greece had already cleared the world of the fantastic images of divinities operating capriciously through natural phenomena." It is fair to infer that the religious element which existed in the minds of these distinguished philosophers did as much to allay an unnatural superstition as it did the scientific part of their teachings; for Religion and Science, when properly united, and acknowledging a belief in the immortality of the soul and the existence of Deity, should be able to make clear to the mind of man the genuine truth, from the fact that both principles are natural and indispensable allies to human progress. It is not to be presumed that all of these philosophers possessed the same sentiments, either upon scientific or religious principles. Socrates had his *Dæmon*, Plato his *Idea*, Aristotle his *Nous;* and the same principle, says Dr. Hitchman, would apply to more modern philosophers. Pritchard would have his *vital principle;* Darwin, the *primordial germ;* Tyndall, the *polar molecules,* and, we may also add, scepticism; Huxley, *his protoplasm;* and Hooker, the *Dionian, carnivorous plant.* Wherever such minds have worked unprejudiced by preconceived dogmatisms, the religious idea has enlightened instead of darkened the human mind in its comprehensions and its illustrations. Professor Tyndall, in speaking of the progress of Science in those days, asks, " What, then, stopped its victorious advance? Why was the scientific intellect compelled, like an exhausted soil, to lie fallow for nearly two millenniums before it could regather the elements necessary to its fertility and strength?" He has answered it better than Bacon or Whewell, so far as it goes. Rome and the other cities of the empire had fallen into moral putrefaction. "Christianity had appeared, offering the Gospel to the poor, and by moderation, if not asceticism of life, practically protesting against the profligacy of the age. The sufferings of the early Christians, and the extraordinary exaltation of mind which enabled them to triumph over the diabolical tortures to which they were subjected, must have left traces not easily effaced. They scorned the earth in view of that building of God, that house not made with hands, eternal in the heavens." The chronology of time happily creates a division, and separates these answers. Will the Professor for a moment contend that the downfall of Rome and other cities of the empire — which he said had fallen into moral putrefaction, the working principles of which preceded the advent and death of Christ — could have been in any manner accelerated by that coming event? Or were not the words "moral putrefaction" sufficient of themselves to cloud and virtually destroy the progress of that Science which had been so brilliant in the before-named ancient cities during the lapse of the last five hundred years before Christ? Does he need any further reasons than those illustrated, as connected with the previous decay of these cities, other than what might exist outside any of the previous sentiments of true Religion, which have ever been taught either before or since?

Does Professor Tyndall contend that Christianity, as a principle, from the day of its birth until the present time, has had anything to do with the want of success in scientific teaching? Has bigotry and superstition, which pure Religion ever rejects, as false claimants to a religious principle, done as much to retard Science as the dogmatism of material scientists has done to retard real Science, or the principles of true Religion co-existent with that age? Again, is not the bigotry as sometimes exemplified by infidel scientists, as strong as any which has ever existed on religious subjects, and would it not, if it had its way, be as severe and cruel in its punishment as that wicked institution, the Inquisition itself?

What though Archbishop Boniface was shocked at the assumption of a world of human beings out of reach of the means of salvation? Or that Augustine, while admitting the rotundity of the earth, would deny the possible existence of inhabitants on the other side, because no such race is recorded in Scripture among the descendants of Adam? Is it remarkable that two good men should suffer their hearts to be the interpreter of their brains, or that they should have chosen what they understood to be a divine law as their guide instead of a material one?

Was the moral or scientific obliquity of Augustine, while comprehending in his age only a part of science, in the admission that the earth was round, though denying a fact in history not revealed to his mind through the code in which he put the most confidence, any greater or more easily shown than in that of the error of the material scientist of to-day, who does not admit a God, or that spirit, in the sense the Christian understands it, has any existence or connection with life and matter?

Is not Prof. Tyndall aware that many of the assumptions of professional scientists, in this age, strike even the educated and practical mind as more absurd than the denial of Augustine, fifteen hundred years ago?

He denied a fact for the want of what he termed inspirational confirmation. Scientists often make great mistakes, as well as assume or adopt improbable conclusions, with all the advantages of education and knowledge which great wealth, and more than two thousand years' experience, have given them. The new and startling assumptions, which are not easily contradicted, are published to the world with all the enthusiasm of a crusader, and they do not deny the reception of homage for the assurance of the dawn of a new truth, even before it is proved.

The discovery of error, though at times important and startling, is not published with much spirit or gusto, but on the other hand is often suffered, like the painful carbuncle, to slough itself slowly off, when the system will bear the poison no longer. In Science, however, the revelations of previous errors affect the whole world, while physical pain may be borne by but one.

We have been taught from childhood that the distance of the earth from the sun was, in round numbers, 95,000,000 of miles; but recently, however, with no additional light upon which to base the real estimate, it has been reduced to 91,000,000. Perhaps with 1875 we shall have still another and a more accurate estimate. In the mean time, little has been said about it by scientists, and less complaint even has been made by educated laymen, though in this change they recognize an enormous difference in the size of the sun and planets, producing its corresponding change in the weight, density, gravity, and attractive and repulsive forces in matter, which of themselves, if taken as a positive, necessary, and invariable standard in the practical application of the industrial arts in the past, would upset the whole system and routine of the social industry of to-day. How does this mysterious but grave error in calculation look alongside of the dispute between two distinguished scientists in Europe, as to whether the retardations of the moon in her revolutions during the past two thousand years have been a sixty-fourth or a thirty-third part of a second of time? On the other hand, it is quite doubtful if in the propagation of any new religious principle, at any age of the world, there was ever, within the same time, an eighth part of the amount of money or mental energy expended as has been during the last five years in advancing and proving the claimed revelations of one single instrument, the spectroscope, used in scientific investigation, the truths or developments of which are yet but very imperfectly proved, to say the least. The spectroscope has taken the world by surprise. Its claimed revelations in Science are marvellous and startling; and though not one person in one hundred, even of the educated classes, as yet understands its mysterious teachings, the world is expected to take it in at once, or, at least, admit its claims on the authority of others, who follow and proclaim its wonders with as much assurance, if not arrogance, as was ever found in any religious reformer since the days of Democritus.

There is mystery with regard to some physical wonders yet to be revealed; these are continually opening, and, strange to say, their discovery is often closely connected with some new necessity of man. Is this chance, or an answer simply to the researches under many daily needs? Or is it a timely revelation of Deity, who comprehends real from imaginary wants, and is ever ready to supply them at the proper time?

Some of the revelations of Science seem only to open a school for intellectual development, while many others provide for the material wants of man.

In the advent of the former is often found elements of speculation which feed the more material mind;

seemingly, however, as yet, they are not closely woven with the needs of society; while in the latter a perfect blending takes place between the understanding and elements of use of cause and effect. We have as yet been denied the knowledge of an open Polar Sea, or the real condition of the Arctic and Antarctic Poles.

Perhaps the necessities of man do not yet require that knowledge; and yet so far as effort is concerned, and the expenditure of money or life, the supposed advantages of such revelation have already been more than counterbalanced. What remains? An impulse seemingly inherent in man to dive into the Poles, and solve the great mystery. We do not know Professor Tyndall's views of what may be revealed there, yet venture the opinion that whatever theories he may adopt as to a solid or open Pole, they would be contradicted by others, and with good reasoning, that may all be done away with when the necessities of man require the knowledge.

ESSAY VII.

SCIENCE AND THE MIDDLE AGES.

Professor Tyndall complains that the religious influence of the Middle Ages was a drawback to scientific progress. But from the days of Democritus to the beginning of the Middle Ages there was a period of nearly one thousand years, at least as eventful as any other equal length of time in the history of the world. During this time occurred the careers of the distinguished leaders from Alexander to Belisarius, with all the changes of government brought about by wars or through political intrigues, with their influences upon Science or the industrial arts, as well as upon Religion; and it is presumed that the human mind was as active and comprehensive as during any other period. From the time of the partition of the Roman Empire, to the establishment of the Eastern or Greek Empire, the learned men or scientists had as much or more to do with the direction, at least in an advisory capacity, as any other class, and were as much responsible for the extremes of intellectual and material aspiration as were the warriors and military leaders. During that period the Greeks placed themselves, in the cultivation of letters and the arts, in the first rank of civilized nations, even if their religious views were not of the sublimest character, or the best suited to perpetuate an age of such material prosperity.

If we should leave Egypt, Syria, Persia, Rome, and Greece behind, with all that was evolved from their history and experience as to the true development of Science and Religion, and for a moment trace the Gauls and Celts across the Alps, with their warlike propensities, appetites, and passions, we find a religious conviction, a belief in the immortality of the soul, and a ruling Deity preceding, but not clouding, their scientific acquirements, and travelling hand in hand in reciprocal progressive impulses. Druids though they were, they early made great progress in the establishment of the true principles of Science and Philosophy, many of which hold good to the present day, — the offspring of their religious impulses, superstitious as they may have been. Their religious festivals directed them to the acquisition of the knowledge of heavenly bodies in the computations of yearly lunations, which gives ground for the opinion that they had knowledge of the solar year. Even in Ireland, relics have been found which are deemed to be astronomical instruments to show the phases of the moon. Astrology, divination, and magic may have been mixed up with their science, as in the case of other nations, yet there is no evidence that this was a result of a religious belief. In medicine they were more superstitious than in other branches of science; and this was nothing new in nationalities of that period, neither is it in our own; for the fundamental principles of medical jurisprudence as an exact law are no better established to-day than they were in the early days of Esculapius. The sacred, mystic character attributed by the Druids to many of the plants indigenous to their own soil, was only equalled by the sublimity of some of their conceptions of cure. The mistletoe was an antidote for all poisons. According to Pliny, as soon as it was discovered upon the oak, the Druids collected in crowds about the tree; a priest in white vestments ascended, and with a knife of gold cut the mistletoe, which was received by another standing on the ground; sacrifices were offered up, and the day spent in rejoicings. All this from a people who were as fierce and warlike as the American savage, and who "hung the heads of the slain in their battles to their horses' manes; while in many of their houses might be seen, nailed up as an heir-loom, the skull of some person of rank who had fallen before them in battle." Such a people, acknowledging a Deity and possessing a religion, as well as a knowledge of some fundamental principles in science, came to civilized and scientific Rome, and for the time overthrew it. Science nearly perished in Rome, but certainly not through any religious fanaticism. "The oppressive rate of interest, the power which the creditors still possessed, and not unfrequently exercised, of life and death over the debtor, had reduced the lower orders to desperation." The instrument of usury is a later and a more piercing instrument to the heart and life of human progress than any principle emanating from true religion. It was not Camillus, the patrician peculator, but Manlius, who through pure feelings of humanity interposed to save Rome. The patricians, however, impeached the latter and sought his death; and a slave treacherously pushed him down the Tarpæan Rock. War and human selfishness in those days had much more to do with the prostration of Science than superstitious belief. It was through the aid of Greek mercenaries that Egypt once again became a Persian province. It was the "progress of the Tarentines in luxury which led to their ruin," which was not less rapid than their advances in literature and refinement.

The barbarisms of Rome disappeared under the influence of the philosophy and literature of Greece, but this was succeeded by the greatest drawback to science the world ever knew. The Romans had extended slavery, that scourge of the East, all over Italy, and slave labor had replaced that of the freeman. It was not Religion that instigated this, but human selfishness, and this brought about the servility of the age. The desolating wars for three centuries preceding the Christian Era were sufficient to crush out nearly all elements of either science or religion that were not grounded upon firm principles, though in the devastating paraphernalia of the wars of that period, much more of science than religion was heard of. Under the new impulse of the Christian religion, more of reverence for Deity and of a higher order became apparent, than had shown itself through the material and dazzling brightness of the civilized and enlightened cities of the East. While politics were working their decrees for nearly five hundred years before the advent of the Middle Ages, or what is termed the Middle Ages, a religious spirit grew up, which tended in its influence to promote scientific investigation wherever an over-zealous fanaticism did not impede its course.

But travelling through the further history of Rome, the whole East, as well as Gaul and Britain and the North Countries, it is fair to claim that religious conviction, a belief in the immortality of the soul and its relations to Deity, did more for true Science than any other impulse not connected with immediate necessities of man in providing his own bread and meat. So that, beginning with the Middle Ages at the sixth century, the evidences of both Science and Religion, as revealed in history, have a fair chance to speak for themselves in the further progress of human life. The natural tendency of the human mind is to extremes and exaggeration; its intuitional and intellectual impulses are often in conflict and at variance in the march for ascendancy and supremacy. This, of course, arises from the predominance of one of these faculties over the other, before the mind becomes balanced under the proper use of each. This conflict is a battle of spirit with matter, in which to a certain extent neither are right, and in which both in the end must make concessions. The brain is the throne from which the practical law for man should be proclaimed, but reason should control. That is the great regulator of a true life. But all the evidence should be brought in before the decision on a line of duty, especially where there is a conflict of purpose. The highest intuitional emotion has its counterpart in material instinct with which to bring up the claims of mind upon matter for judgment; and it is no cloud upon spirit, neither a denial of matter, to say that Divinity is the Author of both, yet demands in a union that harmony of purpose, fitness in action, and end in view which shall ever prove the acknowledgment of infinity in all the relations of life between spirit and matter. Dr. Tyndall's claim for science does not seem to admit this principle. But little can be said favorably of sophists, strictly speaking, either of this or of old Athenian days. Now as then they are often paid for services in upholding the principles of pure selfishness and materialism in some form, which, in the end, prove valuable neither to morals, religion, nor science.

Aristotle needed impressibility, and it was just this lack that would have made him a more enthusiastic religionist. Some of the highest intellectual philosophers, who believed in the immortality of the soul and a religious life, were led more by the material impulses of the intellect than the spiritual, and hence the seeming doubt thrown over their spiritual life. This is true of the present age. What Professor Tyndall terms *imagination*, however, does not account for the lack. It is inspiration, "impressibility," or the influx of a high "spiritual life" to the brain, borrowing force from external instead of internal emotion.

The spread of the Christian religion was opposed by the various governments of the Middle Ages. Churches were early founded in Rome, Corinth, Crete, Antioch, Asia Minor, Britain, and Spain.

Persecution sprang up on every hand, and the revolting spectacles of torture were daily seen in almost every community. "The rage of the Jews brought down the cruel torments of Nero. Some of them," says Tacitus, "were covered over with skins of wild beasts that they might be torn to pieces by dogs; and others were daubed over with combustible materials, and were set up for lights in the night-time, and thus burnt to death." The younger Pliny, in his letter to Trojan, A. D. 107, shows that death was immediately inflicted upon every one who was convicted of belonging to the Christian sect. The wisest and most humane of the heathen emperors was the most fatal to it. During the reign of Maximin, a promiscuous massacre of Christians of all sexes and ages took place. Diocletian demolished the churches and burnt the sacred books. Gallerius continued the persecution with unmitigated severity; "but the fervent spirit of religion was far from yielding to this violent shock." It will be seen from these illustrations that the Christian religion did not darken science, but those who believed in science or patronized it under the old school, were enemies of religion. Still it increased, under all the trials of persecution, and extended through all Europe, where it has since been maintained. From Belisarius to Henry the Eighth, the principal occupation of the world, or at least the leading one, was war. The religious persecutions were against Christianity, and the Christians were not the opposers but the nourishers of science during the Middle Ages. It may properly be said that in some cases heresies of the acknowledged principles of science were suppressed under the dominion of Church rule; this extended but a little way, and towards some who had been leaders in the Church. The mass of the people were free, and acted, so far as their intelligence allowed them, as freely as they do to-day in the exercise of their opinions and belief. It is said of Charlemange that "he was ignorant of the first principles of science till middle age, therefore much could not be expected from him. He gathered about him the learned of every country, and founded an academy," and established laws favorable to the clergy — at that time the sole depositaries and dispensers of learning. The library of Alexandria was destroyed by Arabians, not by Christians. The libraries of Syria shared a like fate. "In the monastic schools" the relics of science found an asylum. The crusades, chivalry, and the Christian religion gave the impulse of advancement, and opened the way to emerge from the Dark Ages. Navigation derived great benefit from the experience necessitated by the crusades, and commerce shared in the gain; while the productions of nature and art, before unknown in the West, called forth fresh industry and new enjoyments. Des Michaels says, "General civilization was advanced by new international relations, and the progress of science and literature. Ideas of honor and courtesy spread from chivalry into society generally, softening the public manners. The advances made by the sciences of geography, history, and medicine were important in giving a new impulse to geographical research and wonder." The invention of the mariners' compass, and the process of manufacturing linen paper, together with the growth of manufactures, fibrous and metallic; the arts of making gunpowder and printing; the discovery of America and the revival of the fine arts, — lit up, as if by magic, the close of the Middle Ages, and laid the foundation of the great scientific improvements of the present age. During the Middle Ages something had been done to dispute the "menial spirit" attributed to them by Professor Tyndall in his quotation of Whewell, "for," says White, "the Church of St. Mark, at Venice, was completed in 1071. Notre Dame, in Paris, was founded in 1163, and occupied one hundred years in building. Westminster Chapel was built in 1220, while from the fall of Charlemagne there was a long period of violence and ignorance during which the Islands of Britain and Ireland claim the honor of sheltering the exiled learning of Europe," while the establishment of Christianity alone preserved the remains of ancient literature, which found a refuge in monastic institutions. Oxford was a flourishing school in about 1200, and Cambridge was incorporated in 1231.

ESSAY VIII.

ATOMIC CONCEPTIONS.

"The strain upon the mind," says Professor Tyndall, "during the stationary period towards ultra-terrestrial things, to the neglect of problems close at hand, was sure to provoke reaction. But the reaction was gradual; for the ground was dangerous, a power being at hand competent to crush the critic who went too far. To elude this power and still allow opportunity for the expression of opinion, the doctrine of 'twofold truth' was invented, according to which an opinion might be held 'theologically' and the opposite opinion 'philosophically.' Thus in the thirteenth century the creation of the world in six days, and the unchangeableness of the individual soul, which had been so distinctly affirmed by St. Thomas Aquinas, were both denied philosophically, but admitted to be true as articles of the Catholic faith. When Protagoras uttered the maxim which brought upon him so much vituperation, that 'opposite assertions are equally true,' he simply meant that human beings differed so much from each other that what was subjectively true to the one might be subjectively untrue to the other. The great sophist never meant to play fast and loose with the truth by saying that one or two opposite assertions, made by the same individual, could possibly escape being a lie. It was not 'sophistry,' but the dread of theologic vengeance, that generated this double-dealing with conviction; and it is astonishing to notice what lengths were possible to men who were adroit in the use of artifices of this kind."

As before remarked, the great strain upon the human mind, during the Middle Ages, was not " ultra-terrestrial," but material. The scientific idea — separate, alone — was very little persecuted by the Church. Where it was pursued outside of that institution and by those who had not been members, little attention was paid to scientific investigation, unless it was considered contradictory of a religious but not a previous scientific faith. Protagoras was banished from Athens as an atheist, not as a scientist; and the maxim of his, that "opposite assertions are equally true," would to-day, if taken literally, prove him such. With Professor Tyndall's explanation of the ancient sophist's meaning, a new construction may be put upon his words. This might also apply to some of Professor Tyndall's ideas, if he thought it of consequence to explain them more fully. It was not the love of science, then, but the dread of the priests, that gave origin to the "twofold truth" set up by the sophists. They were teaching the world to "falsify" through "fear" of persecution. This imputation has sometimes been cast upon the priesthood, with the simple exception that they were to lie for their religion, not for science. Giordano Bruno, the bold philosopher of Italy, was burned for heresy, not for his love for, or belief in, science. The Dominican monk, the pantheist, the disciple of Calvin, and the censurer of monastic institutions, the traducer of what they thought the true church, at last fell under the jealous power of the Inquisition at Venice, which, however, handed him over to the civil powers that had the honor of leading Bruno to the stake.

Are sects charitable towards seceders at the present day? Are scientists forgiving of heresies in their own order? Was animal magnetism recognized or established as a law of science without effort or bitter contradiction? Were the committee of *savans*, appointed by the French government in 1784 to examine the theories of Frederic Anton Mesmer, members of the church? Were they not appointed as distinguished material scientists, opposed to the recognition of spiritual laws? Four physicians, and the distinguished names of Franklin, Leroi, Bailly, DeBory, and Lavoisier, assented to an unfavorable report " not only to the truth of animal magnetism, but to its morality." Were not Jeremy Bentham's philanthropical and philosophical ideas rejected by his peers in legal jurisprudence, while they were more favored by religionists? Have the scientists of Europe or America ever forgiven the justly distinguished Professor Hare of Pennsylvania, or the indefatigable Professor Mapes of New Jersey, for their heresies, in the examination, and final adoption of the principles of Spiritualism, which Professor Tyndall denounces so highly? Has Robert Dale Owen, or Judge Edmonds of New York, fared any better under the scathing blasts of unbelievers, who have not, perhaps, examined any of the phenomena they so studiously investigated? In fact, is dogmatism, fanaticism, jealousy, or persecution any more prevalent in the church than in scientific societies or social unions?

Professor Tyndall further says, "Christendom had become sick of the school of philosophy and its verbal wastes, which led to no issue, but left the intellect in everlasting haze. Here and there he heard the voice of one impatiently crying in the wilderness, 'Not unto Aristotle, not unto subtle hypothesis, not unto Church, Bible, or blind tradition, must we turn for a knowledge of the universe, but to the direct investigation of nature by observation and experiment.'" This is just what had been done in previous ages. Materialists had become disgusted with their own works, as they are always sure to do in time. The productions of Science without Religion are always dry skeletons; they not only lack flesh and blood, but life and motion.

If half the time and money had been expended by the inhabitants of the great cities of the East in rational pursuits, under a proper religious influence, that was devoted to ministering to the intellectual and material senses, both high and low, — the building of huge, unnecessary structures of pride and folly; the ministrations to ambition, jealousy, and animal appetites, where no semblance of spirituality existed or was ever manifest, — it is quite doubtful whether these cities might not have been flourishing to-day, and never have been attacked and destroyed by barbarian invaders. *Christendom* had become sick of Material

Philosophy,— of hewn stones, however large, without cement, of bricks without mortar, of marble images without life, of intellect without soul, of mind without spirit. The thirst was for life, for love, for worship, — for a labor that satisfied the highest ideal of man in his duty to himself and his God. Science ever points out the way, but Religion must travel it with her, never for a moment turning back. They need to go hand in hand; and then life's journey will be, what God designed it, a constant and conscious blessing to man.

Says Sargent: "The unity of all phenomena was the dream of ancient Philosophy. To reduce all this multiplicity of things to a single principle has been, and continues to be, the ever-recurring problem. Water, air, fire, the primary elements, were severally and collectively imagined, by the great thinkers of antiquity, as the original factor.

"To the question of a unity of substance, Greek Science repeatedly applied itself.

"The innumerable varieties in forms, qualities, and habits, in both the vegetable and animal kingdoms, suggest the existence of forces adequate to the production of all the differentiations in nature. Hence to mount to the scientific conception of a single force as the originator and regulator of all these minor forces is the legitimate effort of all profound thought on the subject.

"It was this craving for unity which led the white men of Asia, the ancient Aryan race, to the conception of God as the one substance immanent in the universe. At first they were polytheists, but with the progress of thought their number of gods diminished, and the authors of the Veda at last arrived at the conception of a unity of forces, of a Divine Power as the ultimate substratum of things. They regarded the beings of the world as, in effect, composed of two elements: the one real, of a nature permanent and absolute; the other relative, flowing, variable, and phenomenal; the one matter, the other spirit, but both proceeding from an inseparable unity, a single substance.

"The unity of physical forces is the point on which Science has its eyes now fixed. Materialism is not more eager than Spiritism for the proof. Already has it been demonstrated that heat, electricity, light, magnetism, chemical attraction, muscular energy, and mechanical work, are exhibitions of one and the same power acting through matter. That all these forces may be transformed into motion, and by motion reproduced, is now something more than an hypothesis."

It was the religious spirit which made place for the discoveries of Copernicus, and drew a curtain before the skeleton pictures which had been left of Aristotle. As Professor Tyndall says, "The total crash of Aristotle's closed universe, with the earth at its centre, followed as a consequence; and 'The earth moves!' became a kind of watchword among intellectual freemen." Copernicus was a Christian, be it remembered; Bacon claimed to be; and Descartes rejected the "notion of an atom, because it was absurd to suppose that God, if he so pleased, could not divide an atom." The latter philosopher was at home in material science, but his God was ever present.

"During the Middle Ages," says Tyndall, "the doctrine of atoms had to all appearance vanished from discussion. In all probability it held its ground among sober-minded and thoughtful men, though neither the Church nor the world was prepared to hear of it with tolerance. Once, in the year 1348, it received distinct expression, but retraction by compulsion immediately followed; and thus discouraged, it slumbered till the seventeenth century, when it was revived by a contemporary and friend of Hobbes and Malmesbury, *the orthodox Catholic provost of Digne, Gassendi.*"

Again the Church comes in to help Professor Tyndall carry atoms through the Middle Ages: —

"Referring to the condition of the heathen, who sees a god behind every natural event, thus peopling the world with thousands of beings whose caprices are incalculable, Lange shows the impossibility of any compromise between such notions and those of Science, which proceeds on the assumption of never-changing law and causality. 'But,' he continues, with characteristic penetration, 'when the great thought of one God, acting as a unit upon the universe, has been seized, the connection of things, in accordance with the law of cause and effect, is not only thinkable, but it is a necessary consequence of the assumption. For when I see ten thousand wheels in motion, and know, or believe, that they are all driven by one, then I know that I have before me a mechanism, the action of every part of which is determined by the plan of the whole. So much being assumed, it follows that I may investigate the structure of that machine, and the various motions of its parts. For the time being, therefore, this conception renders scientific action free.'

"Gassendi proceeds, as any heathen might do, to build up the world, and all that therein is, of atoms and molecules. God, who created earth and water, plants and animals, produced, in the first place, a definite number of atoms, which constituted the seed of all things. Then began that series of combinations and decompositions which goes on at present, and which will continue in future. The principle of every change resides in matter. In artificial productions the moving principle is different from the material worked upon; but in nature the agent works within, being the most active and mobile part of the material itself. Thus this bold ecclesiastic, without incurring the censure of the Church or the world, contrives to outstrip Mr. Darwin. The same cast of mind which caused him to detach the Creator from his universe, led him also to detach the soul from the body, though to the body he ascribes an influence so large as to render the soul almost unnecessary."

Professor Tyndall uses a singular argument to prove the independent life of atoms, by beginning, as he has made Gassendi do, in the above few lines, "God, who created earth and water," etc. etc. If the meaning of the Professor is that "In the beginning God created the heaven and the earth, and the earth was without form and void; and darkness was upon the face of the deep. And the spirit of God moved upon the face of the waters," but produced in the first place a definite number of atoms, which constituted the seed of all things, we could not so easily dispute his theory, as it would not be inconsistent with the creation as a whole. We might ask his authority; but the argument, if disputed, would have to be made up of the detail of facts legitimately belonging to Science, without denying the primary Author or the religion of man.

"Accepting here the leadership of Kant," says Tyndall, "I doubt the legitimacy of Maxwell's logic; but it is impossible not to feel the ethic glow with which his lecture concludes. There is, moreover, a very noble strain of eloquence in his description of the steadfastness of the atoms: 'Natural causes, as we know, are at work, which tend to modify, if they do not at length destroy, all the arrangements and dimensions of the earth and the whole solar system. But though in the course of ages catastrophes have occurred and may yet occur in the heavens, though ancient systems may be dissolved and new systems evolved out of their ruins, the molecules out of which these systems are built — the foundation-stones of the material universe — remain unbroken and unworn.'" We disagree with Professor Tyndall on the non-changeableness of molecules. Imponderable molecules are ever changing and never at rest, while the ponderable, or atomic, partake of the same influences of decomposition which apply to all solid, material matter.

"The atomic doctrine, in whole or in part, was entertained by Bacon, Descartes, Hobbes, Locke, Newton, Boyle, and their successors, until the chemical law of multiple proportions enabled Dalton to confer upon it an entirely new significance. In our day there are secessions from the theory, but it still stands firm. Loschmidt, Stoney, and Sir William Thomson have sought to determine the sizes of the atoms, or, rather, to fix the limits between which their sizes lie; while only last year the discourses of Williamson and Maxwell illustrate the present hold of the doctrine upon foremost scientific minds. In fact, it may be doubted whether, wanting this fundamental conception, a theory of the material universe is capable of scientific statement."

It would seem fortunate that the chemical law of "multiple proportions" was discovered in time to enable Dalton to confer upon the "atomic" theory the necessary significance to save the material universe from scientific excommunication.

"The universe is not dead," says Sargent. "Think you this earth of ours is a lifeless, unsentient bulk, while the worm on her surface is in the enjoyment of life? To an inquiry whether the soul is immortal, Apollonius, one of the greatest of the ancient mediums, replied, 'Yes, immortal — but like everything.'

"These suns, systems, planets, and satellites are not mere mechanisms. The pulsations of a divine life throb in them all, and make them rich in the sense that they too are parts of the divine cosmos. Dissolution, disintegration, and change are not death, while an immortal principle survives.

"'Science,' says the Duke of Argyll, 'in the modern doctrine of conservation of energy and the convertibility of forces, is already getting a firm hold of the idea that all kinds of force are but forms of manifestations of one central force issuing from some one fountain-head of power.' Sir John Herschel has not hesitated to say, that '*it is but reasonable to regard the force of gravitation as the direct or indirect result of a consciousness or a will existing somewhere.*'

"Even so orthodox a teacher as President Noah Porter comes up to the vindication of the grand truth, and in vindicating it he has to lend his support to the inevitable doctrine of a spiritual body.

"'The soul,' he says, 'beginning to exist as the principle of life, *may have the power to create other bodies than the physical for itself, or it may already have formed another medium or body in the germ, and may hold it ready for occupation and use as soon as it sloughs off the one which connects it with the earth.* . . . The evidence of observation and of facts is decisive that the soul begins its existence as a vital agency, and emerges by a gradual waking into the conscious activities of its higher nature.'

"The soul which has had enough divine intelligence to prepare for itself a body in this world may be trusted to have ready a fitting substitute when death loosens the physical tie. If from a little microscopic cell, by successive differentiations, it may evolve man's complex organism, surely it may, from its higher point of being, evolve future organisms suited to its more advanced states."

The theory of the creation has been studied for many thousand years; and if the atomic doctrine was really fundamental in establishing the only possible thesis upon which a scientific estimate or exposition could be made, its importance cannot be too highly appreciated. It is possible, however, that some may think that the world, under the Divine Architect, is still governed by fundamental laws, existing prior to the birth of Science in man, and which have not yet been revealed. At any rate, supposed laws have been misunderstood by scientists, much to the discomfort, at times, of the people, who find that the earth " still moves," notwithstanding the predictions of collisions and aberrations that must have destroyed us.

"Ninety years subsequent to Gassendi," says Professor Tyndall, " the doctrine of bodily instruments, as it may be called, assumed immense importance in the hands of Bishop Butler, who, in his famous 'Analogy of Religion,' developed, from his own point of view, and with consummate sagacity, a similar idea. The bishop still influences superior minds; and it will repay us to dwell for a moment on his views. He draws the sharpest distinction between our real selves and our bodily instruments. He does not, as far as I remember, use the word soul, possibly because the term was so hackneyed in his day, as it had been for many generations previously. But he speaks of 'living powers,' 'perceiving' or 'percipient powers,' 'moving agents,' 'ourselves,' in the same sense as we should employ the term soul.

"He dwells upon the fact that limbs may be removed, and mortal diseases assail the body, the mind, almost up to the moment of death, remaining clear. He refers to sleep and to swoon, where the 'living powers' are suspended, but not destroyed. He considers it quite as easy to conceive of existence out of our bodies as in them; that we may animate a succession of bodies, the dissolution of all of them having no more tendency to dissolve our real selves, or 'deprive us of living faculties — the faculties of perception and action — than the dissolution of any foreign matter which we are capable 'of receiving impressions from, or making use of for the common occasions of life.' This is the key of the Bishop's position: 'Our organized bodies are no more a part of ourselves than any other matter around us.' In proof of this he calls attention to the use of glasses, which 'prepare objects' for the 'percipient power' exactly as the eye does."

It is unfortunate that Bishop Butler had not once used the word "soul" in his "Analogy of Religon," which would have cleared all possible doubt in Professor Tyndall's mind of the writer's meaning. This is probably the first time the Bishop's meaning has been mistaken in that respect, or if not mistaken, clouded. A teacher of religion, of world-wide renown, discussing such a question so fully as he did, could have meant nothing else than that spiritual life and intellectual force of mind which survives the body, and claims an immortality beyond the grave. The degree of that life, the measure of the soul in man, or the particular force and mind when connected with the body, as compared to the same principle after the links are severed, of course none can yet tell. But few, however, as before remarked, compared to the millions of millions that have inhabited this earth, have doubted the immortality of the soul, or that its existence while in the body was, to a certain extent, independent and self-operative, while the body itself, except in a mechanical sense, was wholly dependent upon spirit for life and motion. If the body be termed in a literal sense, as it is often called in a figurative sense, a "tenement," it will be easy to illustrate the principle, and answer the query raised by Professor Tyndall in regard to the amputation problem. Suppose, then, that the body be compared to a human house, — a tenement for the habitation of the soul of man. In this house there may be "many mansions" or rooms. It may be a small or a large tenement, without destroying the appropriateness of the illustration for the sizes and capacities of the physical man. The spirit occupies this tenement, — has possession and uses the whole; its capacities for expansion and growth, perhaps enjoyment and usefulness, are dependent upon the size and convenience of the rooms. One of these rooms becomes useless; the spirit no longer occupies it, and withdraws; that part of the tenement is destroyed, leaving other rooms, not so large or convenient perhaps, but comfortable. So another and another in like manner becomes tenantless, and the spirit retires, much to its inconvenience and perhaps its powers of working good. Still it endures till the last room perishes, and then it retires perforce to "a house not made with hands eternal in the heavens." The loss of these respective rooms may be compared to the loss of the limbs of the body; but life exists till the vitals are attacked, and the trunk falls to decay. This is the precise measure of the "bodily instruments" that Science has used, and which Professor Tyndall thinks were so much improved by Bishop Butler. Has any one denied the wonderful mechanism, harmony, and beauty of construction exemplified in the human body, or the adaptability of parts to the whole? Can any one acquainted with its physiology or anatomy for a moment doubt that, from the minutest molecule, globule, nerve, or fibre, up to the comparatively unsensitive human skull, so carefully guarding the throne of reason, there is the least lack of sympathy in every part; or that the smallest jar, disjointure, or decay of one part would not affect the whole body? Yet the wisdom of the Creator has kindly provided that much of all this can be suffered without fatal effects. We would not claim, even, that the spirit, the soul of man, would not be affected, perhaps restrictively, by an amputation of a limb; and that for all time afterwards, till an entire release from the body, its capacity would not be lessened. Bishop Butler speaks of living "powers," "perceiving," "percipient powers," "moving agents," "ourselves"! Why not? Is this inconsistent with the universally claimed attributes of the soul, the mind, the reason of man, as a living consciousness, a unity, yet not taking anything from animal life, but on the contrary, by its independent entity, adding to it?

"The existence," says Sargent, "of a single elementary substance or force, from which, by differentiation, transformation, and the adjustment of proportions, all the varieties and properties of matter are produced, is an hypothesis to which the whole drift of contemporary science is bringing us nearer with every fresh accession of knowledge.

"We know that a very slight change in the arrangement of elemental particles converts wholesome food into poison. Two harmless substances, combined in certain proportions, can produce a deleterious one. Without changing the proportions, a slight change in the molecular arrangement changes properties, — makes the opaque transparent, the palatable unsavory."

It is not claimed that the body itself does not contain for the time being a life principle, though an unconscious one, independent of spirit; but this is only an electric or magnetic force, kept up by actinic molecular action during the time the nerves and tissues are perfect, and before decay takes place. Does it seem at all mysterious that the soul of man forms the conscious motive power or life in the body, while its mysterious and wonderful mechanism may be put in motion, — yea, kept in order by it, through ordinary normal conditions? Is it not possible that conciousness may be lost for a time by some unnatural shock or injury to the body, without annihilating the soul, though it may be unable to remember or express the nature of condition during that time?

"Since the Spirit," says Kardec, "has by his simple will so powerful an action on elementary matter, it may be conceived that he cannot only form substances, but can denaturalize their properties. will having herein the effect of a reagent."

"If, as Liebig, Dumas, and other chemists have asserted, all plants and animals are solidified air, why may not all matter be the product of solidified forces, having their origin in the essence and ultimate reason of things, — in that force and necessity which derive all their virtue from the Divine Idea? This is no fanciful inquiry; its practical interest and importance are brought nearer to us every day by the advance of Science.

"The phenomena here recorded show that matter is not altogether the stuff which our senses would make it appear. 'The force which every being is possessed of,' says Vera, 'as well as the *form* or law according to which it acts and displays its powers, lies in its very nature,' *i. e.,* in its idea. The difference of forces is owing to the difference of ideas. Matter is a force, and the soul is a force, and, as forces, they are the product of one and the same idea, and both produce similar effects; for instance, the soul moves the body, and a body moves another body. Their difference is to be found in their specific elements, or in what constitutes their special idea; for instance, space and time, extent, attraction, and repulsion, etc., for matter; imagination, will, thought, etc., for the soul.

"As idea is force, and the source of all forces, so, if there be no diminution in the quantity of force, it is because its principle, its idea, suffers no deterioration."

THE NEW YORK
PUBLIC LIBRARY

ASTOR, LENOX AND
TILDEN FOUNDATIONS

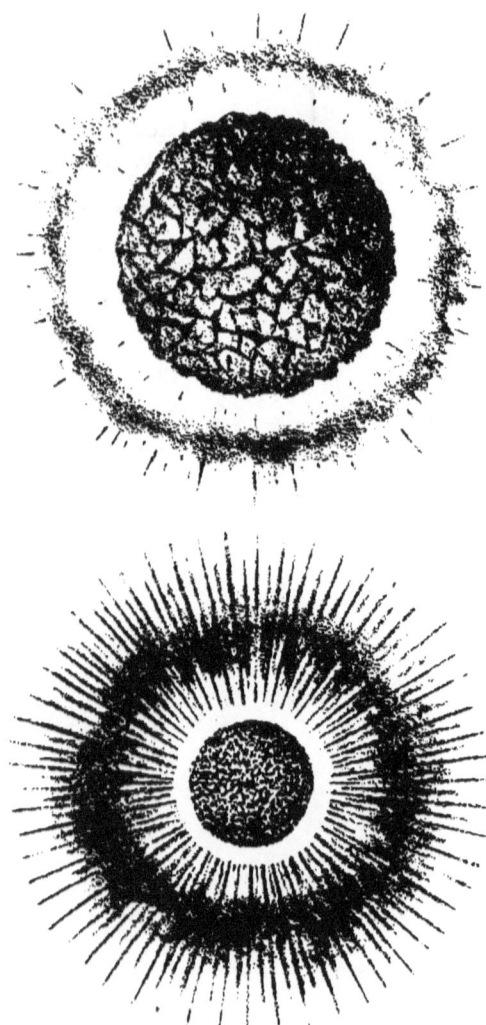

EARTH. PLATE 4.

Plutonic Nucleus of an Earth.

Actienic Nebular Nucleus of an Earth.

ESSAY IX.

MOLECULAR CONSTRUCTION.

THE connection between spirit and matter is mysterious; and while it may be impossible to tell where the influence of the one begins, or that of the other ends, it is equally certain that they both exist.

The electric telegraph cable is stretched across the Atlantic Ocean, and we converse through it. We know that the wire is a simple conductor, and that electricity is the messenger. Without either of these the intelligence which we receive could not come across this vast expanse of water, in an almost incredibly short time, although the force or conscious life principle would still be there. Consciousness exists in us as the secondary embodied agents, while we receive it from the great primary God himself. We could not act without him. The wires would not work intelligently without human agency, which shows that the spirit is in and through all things material. The agent connecting Duxbury with Brest lies like a gorged serpent, till the key is touched at either end by an intelligent hand, and a spark flies off sending knowledge broadcast over the world. Seemingly no force or life exists in the wires till vent is given to the electric spark, when, so sensitive is the force, the minutest line is mechanically traced, showing a maximum or minimum power in its touch that the human eye alone could not comprehend. So when the circulation of blood is stopped in the human body, sensation practically ceases, but revives again with motion in the heart. We may sleep, we may swoon or be entranced, and be insensible to pain; but our "living powers" are not destroyed, only suspended. The human mind itself is conscious that the body is only its "tenement," as it requires intelligence to move even a finger; yet all this time the functions of animal life are working within, almost unconscious to ourselves.

We can here safely repeat the position of Bishop Butler, as quoted by Professor Tyndall, reserving only "the spirit within us." "Our organized bodies are no more a part of ourselves than any other matter around us." Why should they be? Are we not daily sustained and recuperated? Are not our wasting muscles daily renewed by matter? Professor Tyndall interposes an imaginary dialogue between Bishop Butler and Lucretius, which adds but little to the illustration of his argument. Speaking for the Bishop to Lucretius, he says, "May I ask you, then, to try your hand upon this problem? Take your dead hydrogen-atoms, your dead oxygen-atoms, your dead carbon-atoms, your dead nitrogen-atoms, your dead phosphorus-atoms, and all the other atoms, dead as grains of shot, of which the brain is formed. Imagine them separate and sensationless, observe them running together and forming all imaginable combinations. This, as a purely mechanical process, is *seeable* by the mind. But can you see, or dream, or in any way imagine, how out of that mechanical act, and from these individually dead atoms, sensation, thought, and emotion are to arise? Are you likely to extract Homer out of the rattling of dice, or the Differential Calculus out of the clash of billiard balls? I am not all bereft of this *Vorstellungs-kraft* of which you speak; nor am I, like so many of my brethren, a mere vacuum as regards scientific knowledge. I can follow a particle of musk until it reaches the olfactory nerve; I can follow the waves of sound until their tremors reach the water of the labyrinth, and set the otoliths and Corti's fibres in motion; I can also visualize the waves of ether as they cross the eye and hit the retina. Nay, more, I am able to pursue to the central organ the motion thus imparted at the periphery, and to see in idea the very molecules of the brain thrown into tremors. My insight is not baffled by these physical processes. What baffles and bewilders me is the notion that from those physical tremors things so utterly incongruous with them as sensation, thought, and emotion can be derived. You may say, or think, that this issue of consciousness from the clash of atoms is not more incongruous than the flash of light from the union of oxygen and hydrogen."

A few questions differing from the above (which have already been answered) may pertinently be asked Professor Tyndall, as they are directly in his line: Why will ice congeal in the fall of the year at the same temperature of atmosphere in which it will melt in the spring? Why will a drop of water outweigh the atmosphere more than seven hundred times, when the constituent parts of oxygen and hydrogen in the same drop, if separated, are much lighter than the atmosphere? Why will vapor, theoretically heavier specifically than the atmosphere, float for days above our heads without falling? Why will the heat of the sun, which as heat must be much lighter than common air, penetrate a belt around the earth of some fifty miles in thickness, and preserve itself as heat, though flowing down through a strata of intensely increasing cold at every given point above the earth's surface? In the history of science, why has Newton been made to say that light was composed of colors, when he said directly to the contrary? Why is the theory of undulation, as a simple transmissive process, credited to Young, when it was Newton who first mentioned light as moving in waves? Why are the corpuscles named by Newton in connection only with his theory of colors used improperly to illustrate his theory of light? Professor Tyndall says for Bishop Butler, in answering Lucretius, that "you cannot satisfy the human understanding in its demand for logical continuity between molecular processes and the phenomena of consciousness." For this he deserves much credit.

"Chemistry," says Sargent, " by its theory of equivalents, is tending to unity. Few intelligent chemists now regard the elements ranked as simple as being simple any further than the present imperfection of our instruments compels us to class them as such. The employment of the balance has demonstrated that in the chemical transformations of bodies, nothing is created, nothing is lost.

"Hence the sum of the material elements is constant, and, as it is impossible to conceive a limit to the universe, this sum is infinite; and thus the aspects so various which matter presents consist only in the *forms* it successively takes on according to the combinations of its chemical elements.

"But the substance of things evades all chemical testing; and so the simple bodies of Chemistry are themselves only forms, more or less elementary, the agglomeration of which produces compounds.

"If by the theory of equivalents these forms should be some day reduced to unity, *Chemistry* will be entitled to infer, with some reason, the substantial unity of the universe.

"Neither the primitive cell, regarded as an elementary form of life, nor any principle known to Science, suffices to explain life itself, or that power of action which is in the living being at all the epochs of its existence, and consequently in the cell. In addition, therefore, to the material and sensible elements, there must be in it a principle inaccessible to observation; and it is this principle which is the agent of life, the impelling cause of vital motion and of all differentiations.

"But the reduction of all living forms to unity, that is, to the cell, is an indication that the vital agent is itself a form of the one primitive force, and thus *Physiology* tends to unity by the way of Morphology; and this reduction of organs to unity may be proved for plants as well as for animals.

"The unity of the principle of life and thought is another conclusion to which science is tending in the department of Physiology. Every primary germ owes its evolution to the spirit or idea involved. If the cell is the most elementary form of the living being, the principle of life which it encloses cannot be developed except in so far as the form at which it ought to arrive *resides in it already in the state of idea.* This idea expands with the life, ramifies with it, accommodates itself to the means and conditions which the general order of the universe imposes; and *thus the study of the psychical nature of man* points also in the direction of unity.

"The embryo is preserved by intelligent processes of which neither itself nor its parents know anything. This intelligence is a property of the life by which they live.

"This life, what is it but the pervading efflux of the Deific love and life vivifying all nature and sustaining the animal and vegetable world as well as the world of mind?

"Should it be objected that this proves too much; that it involves the identity of the vital principle of animals and vegetables, let us not shrink from the conclusion. The essential unity of all spirit and all life with this exuberant life from God is a truth from which we need not recoil, even though it bring all animal and vegetable forms within the sweep of immortality."

Bishop Butler's work able as it is, failed to satisfy the materialists, probably because behind all his structures there existed the idea of life, and that life-force was spirit. He has been eclipsed by modern scientists in his perceptions and delineations of the æsthetic domain of the naturalists. The geological record has been much enlarged, the domain of physics has been extended, till science and sociology have few barriers between.

To use the words of Tyndall, " The rigidity of old conceptions has been relaxed, the public mind being rendered gradually tolerant of the idea that not for six thousand, nor for sixty thousand, nor for six thousand thousand thousand, but for æons embracing untold millions of years, this earth has been the theatre of life and death. The riddle of the rocks has been read by the geologist and paleontologist, from the subcambrian depths to the deposits thickening over the sea-bottoms of to-day. And upon the leaves of that stone book are, as you know, stamped the characters, plainer and surer than those formed by the ink of history, which carry the mind back into abysses of past time compared with which the periods which satisfied Bishop Butler cease to have a visual angle.

" The lode of discovery once struck, those petrified forms in which life was at one time active increased to multitudes and demanded classification. They were grouped in genera, species, and varieties, according to the degree of similarity subsisting between them. Thus confusion was avoided, each object being found in the pigeon-hole appropriated to it, and to its fellows of similar morphological or physiological character. The general fact soon became evident that none but the simplest forms of life lie lowest down, that as we climb higher among the superimposed strata, more perfect forms appear. . . . De Maillet, a contemporary of Newton, has been brought into notice by Professor Huxley as one who 'had a notion of the modifiability of living forms.'

"In my frequent conversations with him, the late Sir Benjamin Brodie, a man of highly-philosophic mind, often drew my attention to the fact that, as early as 1794, Charles Darwin's grandfather was the pioneer of Charles Darwin. In 1801, and in subsequent years, the celebrated Lamarck, who produced so profound an impression on the public mind through the vigorous exposition of his views by the author of the 'Vestiges of Creation,' endeavored to show the development of species out of changes of habit and external condition. In 1813 Dr. Wells, the founder of our present theory of dew, read before the Royal Society a paper, in which, to use the words of Mr. Darwin, 'he distinctly recognizes the principle of natural selection; and this is the first recognition that has been indicated.'

"These papers were followed in 1859 by the publication of the first edition of 'The Origin of Species.' All great things come slowly to the birth. Copernicus, as I informed you, pondered his great work for thirty-three years. Newton for nearly twenty years kept the idea of gravitation. . . .

"It is conceded on all hands that what are called varieties are continually produced. The rule is probably without exception. No chick and no child is in all respects and particulars the counterpart of its brother and sister; and in such differences we have 'variety' incipient. No naturalist could tell how far this variation could be carried; but the great mass of them held that never, by any amount of internal or external change, nor by the mixture of both, could the offspring of the same progenitor so far deviate from each other as to constitute different species. The function of the experimental philosopher is to combine the conditions of Nature and to produce her results; and this was the method of Darwin. He made himself acquainted with what could, without any manner of doubt, be done in the way of producing variation. . . .

"We cannot, without shutting our eyes through fear or prejudice, fail to see that Darwin is here dealing, not with imaginary, but with true causes; nor can we fail to discern what vast modifications may be produced by natural selection in periods sufficiently long. Each individual increment may resemble what mathematicians call a 'differential' (a quantity indefinitely small); but definite and great changes may obviously be produced by the integration of these infinitesimal quantities through practically infinite time.

"If Darwin, like Bruno, rejects the notion of creative power acting after human fashion, it certainly is not because he is unacquainted with the numberless exquisite adaptations on which this notion of a supernatural artificer has been founded."

Mr. Darwin's theories are not now specially under discussion; and if they were, it would not be necessary in this connection to say more than that there is ever recognized behind them a "Divinity," a life-spirit force, which would always relieve them from the charge of self-existent Materialism. The "Origin of Species" acknowledges an originator, lying always beyond mere physical laws. Even if Mr. Darwin is correct in his sliding scale of improved organism, it does not by any means prove that the origin of that measure of development is physical evolution merely. The spiritual law may have as much to do with animal progression, as the special physiological developments described by Mr. Darwin. It is plain that the physical evolution of animals cannot be carried on without life, and that the origin of that life is spirit. Until animal life is found without spirit, and is developed independent of spirit force, it is foolish to strive to draw intelligent distinctions between the relative progressive powers of each in the development of animal life.

"'Living beings,' says Stirling, 'do exist in a mighty chain from the moss to the man; but that chain, far from founding, is founded *in* the idea, and is not the result of any mere natural *growth* into this or that. That chain is itself the most brilliant stamp and sign-manual of design."

"Even granting," says Vera, "that the germ be endowed with an inexhaustible power of begetting similar individuals, or that it should contain, like some infinitesimal quantity, an infinite number of germs, such hypotheses will explain neither the initial germ, nor the unity of the species, nor even the grown-up and complete individual. . . . The idea must constitute the common stock, and the ultimate principle to which the individual, the species, and the genus, owe their origin and existence."

"*Thought is a motion of matter*," says Moleschott. But this is no more an explanation than would be an attempt to account for the sentiment and the charm in a melody of Mozart's by saying, "It is a motion of matter." All that Science can fairly hypothecate is, that *thought is accompanied by a motion of matter;* for were the head and brain so transparent that this motion could be seen, the mystery of thought would be as far as ever from being solved.

"Mr. Tyndall," says Sargent, "would trace all the phenomena of mind and matter to the potencies of atoms. He allows Theism, however, to entertain its little hypothesis, and leaves it an open question whether atoms may not have had a Divine Creator.

"'Abandoning all disguise,' he says, 'the confession I feel bound to make before you is, that I prolong the vision backward across the boundary of the experimental evidence, and discern in that matter which we, in our ignorance, and notwithstanding our professed reverence for its Creator, have hitherto covered with opprobrium, *the promise and potency of every form and quality of life.*'"

"I agree with Mr. Tyndall that there is nothing very alarming in the mild and contradictory Materialism that would not exclude the postulate of a Creator behind and beyond matter. His 'confession' is not a startling one, either to the materialist or the spiritist; for it is an attempt to sit at the same time on the stools of both; nor is it striking for its novelty."

"In our day," says Tyndall, "grand generalizations

have been reached. The theory of the origin of species is but one of them. Another, of still wider grasp and more radical significance, is the doctrine of the Conservation of Energy, the ultimate philosophical issues of which are as yet but dimly seen — that doctrine which 'binds Nature fast in fate' to an extent not hitherto recognized, exacting from every antecedent its equivalent consequent, from every consequent its equivalent antecedent, and bringing vital as well as physical phenomena under the dominion of that law of causal connection which, so far as the human understanding has yet pierced, asserts itself everywhere in nature. Long in advance of all definite experiment upon the subject, the constancy and indestructibility of matter had been affirmed; and all subsequent experience justified the affirmation. Later researches extended the attribute of indestructibility to force. This idea, applied in the first instance to inorganic, rapidly embraced organic nature.

"The vegetable world, though drawing almost all its nutriment from invisible sources, was proved incompetent to generate anew either matter or force. Its matter is for the most part transmuted gas; its force transformed solar force. The animal world was proved to be equally uncreative, all its motive energies being referred to the combustion of its food. The activity of each animal as a whole was proved to be the transferred activity of its molecules. The muscles were shown to be stores of mechanical force, potential until unlocked by the nerves, and then resulting in muscular contractions. The speed at which messages fly to and fro along the nerves was determined, and found to be, not, as had been previously supposed, equal to that of light or electricity, but less than the speed of a flying eagle.

"This was the work of the physicist; then came the conquests of the comparative anatomist and physiologist, revealing the structure of every animal, and the function of every organ in the whole biological series, from the lowest zoöphyte up to man. The nervous system had been made the object of profound and continued study, the wonderful and, at bottom, entirely mysterious controlling power which it exercises over the whole organism, physical and mental, being recognized more and more. Thought could not be kept back from a subject so profoundly suggestive. Besides the physical life dealt with by Mr. Darwin, there is a psychical life presenting similar gradations, and asking equally for a solution. How are the different grades and orders of mind to be accounted for? What is the principle of growth of that mysterious power which on our planet culminates in reason? These are questions which, though not thrusting themselves so forcibly upon the attention of the general public, had not only occupied many reflecting minds, but had been formerly broached by one of them before 'The Origin of Species' appeared."

"Let us suppose that Darwinism is triumphant at every point. Imagine it to be demonstrated that the long line of our genealogy can be traced back to the lowest organisms; suppose that our descent from the ape is conclusively proved, and the ape's descent from the tidal animal, and the tidal animal's descent from some ultimate monad, in whom all the vital functions are reduced to the merest rudiments. Or, if we will, let us suppose that a still further step has been taken, and the origin of life itself discovered, so that, by putting a certain mixture in an hermetically-sealed bottle, we can create our own ancestors over again. When we endeavor firmly to grasp that conception, we are, of course, sensible of a certain shock. We have a prejudice or two derived from the Zoölogical Gardens and elsewhere, which, as it were, causes our gorge to rise; but when we have fairly allowed the conception to sink into our minds, when we have brought our other theories into harmony with it, and have lost that uncomfortable sense of friction and distortion which is always produced by the intrusion of a new set of ideas, what is the final result of it all? What is it that we have lost, and what have we acquired in its place? It is surely worth while to face the question boldly, and look into the worst fears that can be conjured up by these terrible discoverers. Probably, after such an inspection, the thought that will occur to any reasonable man will be, What does it matter? What possible difference can it make to me whether I am sprung from an ape or an angel? The one main fact is that, somehow or other, I am here. How I came here may be a very interesting question to speculative persons, but my thoughts and sensations and faculties are the same on any hypothesis. Sunlight is just as bright if the sun was once a nebulous mass.

"The convenience of our arms and legs is not in the

slightest degree affected by the consideration that our great-great-grandfathers were nothing better than more or less movable stomachs. The poet's imagination and the philosopher's reason are none the worse because the only sign of life given by their ancestors was some sort of vague contractility in a shapeless jelly. Our own personal history, if we choose to trace it far enough back, has taken us through a series of changes almost equally extensive, and we do not think any the worse of ourselves on that account. Our affections and our intellectual faculties are in existence. They are the primary data of the problem, and as long as we are conscious of their existence we need not worry ourselves by asking whether they began to exist by some abrupt change, or gradually rose into existence through a series of changes. There is still quite as much room as ever for the loftiest dreams that visit the imaginations of saints or poets." *

The material law, as contra-distinguished from the spiritual, would ever lead the world astray by technical demand; the spiritual, if taken by itself, would lead to an extreme generalization. Each of these, when acting as independent forces, would be imperative in their sway. The proper life for man is a modification of each law in the development of individual existence. In proportion as either extreme is tolerated, the mind becomes affected, and the life becomes co-operative in the result. It may be inferred from the experiences of

---

* Correspondence of "Popular Science Monthly" for June, 1872.

life, that the spirit-forces within us are imbued with heavenly longings to an extent hardly controllable or practicable with the duties of material life on this earthly sphere; while, on the other hand, the animal in man, if suffered to vent itself unrestrained, would soon reduce him to a grovelling, sensual being, impracticable in his emotional thought and action for any enjoyment and usefulness in life. If we can draw any safe conclusion from the law of our whole being, it is that in human life these two laws must be united; and so united, they work out for us a new existence, higher, stronger, and more individual in its essence, and more independent in its entity than the pre-existing life-forces in man possessed, and that this principle is immortal. The intellect of man is furnished him by the Creator as the great regulator of the workings of animal and spirit life.

"If Mr. Tyndall means merely to repeat Locke," says Sargent, "and say that all that he would suggest is, that matter may be *divinely* impressed with the power of generating mind, then he at once spiritualizes matter and lowers the flag of Materialism.

"But this is not what he means. When he tells us that matter may contain 'the promise and potency of every form and quality of life,' what he means, obviously, is that, among other qualities of life which mere matter may involve, is that of mind. Now, this idea has been often put forth, long before Mr. Tyndall's day, and as often answered. By no one has it been answered better than by Schelling (1775–1854), who said of the attempts in his day to make matter account for *all* the phenomena of life, 'To explain *thinking* as a material phenomenon is possible only in this way: that we reduce matter itself to a spectre, — to the mere modification of an intelligence whose common functions are thinking and matter.'

"Coleridge, who was accustomed to borrow from Schelling, expresses the same idea thus, and his words fully answer all that Mr. Tyndall has to say about matter: 'As soon as Materialism becomes intelligible, it ceases to be Materialism. In order to explain *thinking* as a material phenomenon, it is necessary to refine matter into a mere modification of intelligence, with the twofold function of *appearing* and *perceiving*. Even so did Priestley in his controversy with Price.' (Even so would Tyndall do now!) 'He stripped matter of all its material properties, substituted spiritual powers, and when we expected to find a body, behold! we had nothing but its ghost — the apparition of a defunct substance!'

"'To say that matter is the principle of all things,' remarks Paul Janet, 'is simply equivalent to saying we do not know what is the principle of all things, — a very luminous science, indeed! Even in its claim that matter is eternal, Materialism has to beg its premises, and to proceed wholly on a metaphysical, *à priori* assumption. If Materialism does not explain matter, much less does it explain mind and thought.'

The "practical man" is as much the work of a divine law, as spirit or matter in their separate entities. This includes all there is of man in his spiritual, intellectual, or physical existence. The work of life is this development; it is an imperative law of divinity — man's plans to the contrary, nevertheless. Life teaches stern lessons, which in our choice we would avoid, but cannot. Thus spirit and matter are modifiers of each other, and the life beyond the grave must be higher, stronger, better, for its conflict with the material life here. Inspiration comes from the spirit; desire, from the impulses of both body and mind. Fate is not inexorable, but can be modified by practical observances. Force is indestructible, but changing, and vents itself always in the weakest spot. Fate has always weak points that can be turned against itself. The vegetable world, while apparently drawing its life from 'invisible sources,' partakes largely of the same elements as animal life. Matter is the slag of imponderable molecular workings; spirit life and electric life develop psychical force; and all these in their action unite in making a Science of Sociology.

ESSAY X.

SCIENCE AND SOCIOLOGY.

The present may be considered a generation peculiar to itself. At no period in the earth's history, so far as we can judge, has there been so much to constitute a peculiarly independent and enlightened people, either from the physical, mental, or spiritual controlling influences that surround them, as during the nineteenth century.

That all-prevailing active principles of evolution have their influence, for the time being, in the formation of the man of his especial day, none can doubt; and it is only from a full comprehension of rapidly-changing associations which surround him that we can realize what he is or really ought to be. The common laborer, the mechanic, the merchant, or professional man of the first part of this century found himself encompassed and controlled by entirely different influences from those living in the Middle Ages, rendering it not only proper, but imperative, that he should find new means and methods of carrying on his avocation or profession, or find himself practically superseded by others following in his track, of more recent light and experience.

The necessary changes in the education and pursuits of a second generation are hardly less, while those of the third and the fourth may be still more difficult to overcome.

The printing-press, the steam-engine, the electric telegraph, and other mechanical appliances have not only produced a marked change, and facilitated ways and means of doing business and gaining a livelihood, but have quickened and enlarged the capacity and habit of thought in accomplishing life's duties. If the compass and strength of mentality have not increased, they certainly have been wonderfully quickened.

Religious, scientific, political, and social teachings are weighed more by the people than ever before; and although the observable results at the present moment exist rather in the shape of protests and demurrings than in any other form, it is probable that positive and systematic action on the part of the masses will soon follow with telling effect, in creating new and still wider spheres of active life, working upon new principles of individual effort, — these principles recognizing the fact, that to the laws of life belong the laws of government, both of man's passions and energies, and the more collective principles of aggregate municipality.

The scientific world is no exception to these popular changes. The law of constructive aggregation is recognized by the physicist of the present day as running from the entity of spiritual life, through molecular and atomic conditions, to the completed creations of the universe. Each in turn projects theories of vital, practical forces to be controlled by human organisms for the development of mankind, and claims a knowledge of the specific relations of mind and matter to accomplish these objects. In the magnitude and beauty of his conceptions, he sometimes forgets or neglects the relative conditions of caste, through which omission conflicts occasionally arise.

These concussions of energies happily are growing less, as the two planes of evolution approach each other. For if the artisan is growing wiser, the cloak of professional exclusiveness is becoming threadbare; and he who would now be thought wise in his calling, as he may ever desire to be, is learning to throw his exclusiveness off, that his true merit may become known through his simplicity and frankness, the best hope of success in life.

With the professional physicist there has been change and much improvement; but great defects, which should be remedied, still exist in his system of acquiring, as well as teaching. Individual thought and investigation with him is properly becoming more a habit, and he trusts less to others in working out his theories for the practical world; while formulas known only to connoisseurs are being laid aside in addresses to the people, who are, after all, the real supports of science.

The laws of Science are as applicable to Sociology as to the physical creation. The vital scientist of to-day is the one who sees the need of as much philosophy in the daily manipulations and mechanical and muscular labors of the artisan, as in the laws of attraction and gravitation of physical matter. With such, life is not mere animal or mental existence, but a leverage for moving the conditions of eternity; to live, to accomplish is his work; and his aim is to subvert all such antagonistic forces as would pervert the highest progress of man.

The professional is no less dependent in his sphere; for his very life — culture, experience, and ability to enjoy, communicate, or teach — depends upon the drafts he makes upon the muscles, the brain, or the intellect of laborer, artisan, and merchant, in their several callings.

The majority of muscular forces is the majority of numbers, not always in the right, but capable of becoming so if influenced by intellectual and spiritual culture; and tests of truth and reality would be, in such cases, the safest standard for government. Humanitarian moralists often lose, if they have ever attained, the practical knowledge of character in their ideal estimate of moral accountability; while the people, possessed of the better practical knowledge, may be deficient in due estimate of the higher qualities: so idealists depend too much on the efforts of practical men, and the latter, in turn, do not cultivate with emotional fervor the elevated ideas of the former.

It may be the united and fortunate work of the present age to reconstruct industrial life, as science is being reconstructed. Certainly there never was more need of a union and modification of all social and scientific elements or of practical cohesion. The mere universal effort towards this union would at least lead to a fuller and better understanding of all the workings of mind and matter, the studious combinations of human and mechanical energies for the better provision of industrial art, the muscular and mental development of daily labor, and the thoroughly practical tendencies of the professional sciences.

"With," says Tyndall, "the mass of materials furnished by the physicist and physiologist in his hands, Mr. Herbert Spencer, twenty years ago, sought to graft upon this basis a system of psychology, and two years ago a second and greatly amplified edition of his work appeared. Those who have occupied themselves with the beautiful experiments of Plateau will remember that, when two spherules of olive-oil, suspended in a mixture of alcohol and water of the same density as the oil, are brought together, they do not immediately unite; something like a pellicle appears to be formed around the drops, the rupture of which is immediately followed by the coalescence of the globules into one. There are organisms whose vital actions are almost as purely physical as that of those drops of oil. They come into contact and fuse themselves thus together. From such organisms to others a shade higher, and from these to others a shade higher still, and on through an ever-ascending series, Mr. Spencer conducts his argument. There are two obvious factors to be here taken into account, — the creature and the medium in which it lives, or, as it is often expressed, the organism and its environment. Mr. Spencer's fundamental principle is that between these two factors there is incessant interaction. The organism is played upon by the environment, and is modified to meet the requirements of the environment. Life he defines to be 'a continuous adjustment of internal relations to external relations.'"

The spiritual and physical type of man, and their evolution and development, find a correspondence in the molecular energy and construction of animate and inanimate physical matter.

The instinct of labor-saving processes, as well as knowledge for utilizing life's duties and means of support, prompts to a ceaseless investigation to control the powers of nature for our own practical purposes; and though culture and experience may enhance or enlarge such desires, they are not confined to that condition of mind. With this instinctive ability of the human soul, together with the enlightened opportunities for experience afforded to all at the present day, there is little excuse for ignorance, on the part of any class of people, of the fundamental principles involving our earthly existence, and its full and happy development; and certainly there is no reason why teachings from each sphere or standpoint should not be received in sympathy by such as occupy stations superior or inferior to any given position, without jealousy or envious misappropriation.

In the normal energies of each there is neither haste nor waste, but constant progressive action. Concentrated existence is the highest conception of both material and spiritual force and energy, with all their infinite and finite mental or mechanical conditions of matter beyond. The human system, with all its characteristics accompaniments of physical strength or weakness, intellectuality or imbecility, beauty or ugliness, must have been, and is now, subject to the same strange, accidental changes in construction and condition that the more earthy substances of our globe exhibit at the present time.

"Combining such facts," says Tyndall, "with the doctrine of hereditary transmission, we reach a theory of instinct. A chick, after coming out of the egg, balances itself correctly, runs about, picks up food, thus showing that it possesses a power of directing its movements to definite ends. How did the chick learn this very complex co-ordination of eye, muscles, and beak? It has not been individually taught; its personal experience is *nil;* but it has the benefit of ancestral experience. In its inherited organization are registered all the powers which it displays at birth."

Rather might we say, in its instinctive organization there is furnished by the Creator a means of life not given to the child of man. When we ask what instinct is, we find the natural answer running through all the animal creation, *Impressibility.* No material organization, of its own volition, could provide the ways and means of life or safety shown through the instinct of the animal creation; and the intelligence and foresight shown by them proves that there is a superior intelligence above and around, constantly impressing them to action that could not be accounted for through any laws of physical inheritance.

There is in every organized being an infinite world of the most various actions going on. The forces penetrating us are as manifold as the material we are moulded from. In every point of our bodies, and at every moment of our existence, all the energies of nature meet and unite. Yet such order rules in the course of these wonderful workings, that harmonious, blended action, instead of bewildering confusion, characterizes beings endowed with life. Everything in them commands and answers with balance and counterpoise. Buffon long ago felt and expressed this. The animal, he said, combines all the forces of nature; his individuality is a centre to which everything is referred, a point reflecting the whole universe, a world in little, — a profound saying coming from the great naturalist as the flash of an intuition of genius, rather than the result of rigid investigation; words which the movement of Science confirms with ever stronger proofs, while borrowing from them light for its path. Thus the connecting links between mind and matter are established, and the electric and magnetic currents seem the medium of their united action.

We assume that psycho-animal life is progressively regenerative, yet it may be doubted whether the physico-normal man has materially changed since the creation, except in a regular line of development; while spirit may have migrated, through all time, from one physical constitution to another, aggregating the elements of human life and growth in each and every evolution, till the more perfect development of man is attained. In the material evolution of an earth the actinic influences — which may be termed the soul of matter — are ever at work in construction of multiple forces and aggregated combinations, which move onward to the final development, in like manner as the soul and intellect of man, in their own line of progression, carry him forward to a higher and more complete existence.

Says Tyndall, "Man also carries with him the physical texture of his ancestry, as well as the inherited intellect bound up with it. The defects of intelligence during infancy and youth are probably less due to a lack of individual experience, than to the fact that in early life the cerebral organization is still incomplete. The period necessary for completion varies with the race and with the individual. As a round shot outstrips a rifled one on quitting the muzzle of the gun, so the lower race in childhood may outstrip the higher; but the higher eventually overtakes the lower, and surpasses it in range. As regards individuals, we do not always find the precocity of youth prolonged to mental power in maturity, while the dulness of boyhood is sometimes strikingly contrasted with the intellectual energy of after-years. Newton, when a boy, was weakly, and he showed no particular aptitude at school; but in his eighteenth year he went to Cambridge, and soon afterward astonished his teacher by his power of dealing with geometrical problems. During his quiet youth his brain was slowly preparing itself to be the organ of those energies which he subsequently displayed.

"Throughout this application and extension of the 'Law of Inseparable Associations,' Mr. Spencer stands upon his own ground, invoking, instead of the experiences of the individual, the registered experiences of the race. His overthrow of the restriction of experience to the individual is, I think, complete. That restriction ignores the power of organizing experience furnished at the outset to each individual; it ignores the different degrees of this power possessed by different races and by different individuals of the same race. Were there not in the human brain a potency antecedent to all experience, a dog or cat ought to be as capable of education as a man. These predetermined internal relations are independent of the experiences of the individual. The human brain is the 'organized register of infinitely numerous experiences received during the evolution of life, or rather during the evolution of that series of organisms through which the human organism has been reached. The effects of the most uniform and frequent of these experiences have been successively bequeathed, principal and interest, and have slowly mounted to that high intelligence which lies latent in the brain of the infant. Thus it happens that the European inherits from twenty to thirty cubic inches more of brain than the Papuan. Thus it happens that faculties, as of music, which scarcely exist in some inferior races, become congenital in superior ones. Thus it happens that out of savages unable to count up to the number of their fingers, and speaking a language containing only nouns and verbs, arise at length our Newtons and Shakespeares.'

"Divorced from matter, where is life to be found? Whatever our *faith* may say, our *knowledge* shows them to be indissolubly joined. Every meal we eat, and every cup we drink, illustrates the mysterious control of mind by matter.

"We need clearness and thoroughness here. Two courses, and two only, are possible: either let us open our doors freely to the conception of creative acts, or, abandoning them, let us radically change our notions of matter.

"The 'Materialism' here professed may be vastly different from what you suppose, and I therefore crave your gracious patience to the end. 'The question of an external world,' says Mr. J. S. Mill, 'is the great battle-ground of metaphysics.' Mr. Mill himself reduces external phenomena to 'possibilities of sensation.' Kant, as we have seen, made time and space 'forms' of our own intuitions. Fichte, having first, by the inexorable logic of his understanding, proved himself to be a mere link in that chain of eternal causation which holds so rigidly in Nature, violently broke the chain by making Nature, and all that it inherits, an apparition of his own mind.

"That anything answering to our impressions exists outside of ourselves is not a *fact*, but an *inference*, to which all validity would be denied by an idealist like Berkeley or by a sceptic like Hume. Mr. Spencer takes another line. With him, as with the uneducated man, there is no doubt or question as to the existence of an external world.

"Considered fundamentally, then, it is by the operation of an insoluble mystery that life on earth is evolved, species differentiated, and mind unfolded from their prepotent elements in the immeasurable past. There is, you will observe, no very rank Materialism here.

"The strength of the doctrine of evolution consists, not in an experimental demonstration (for the subject is hardly accessible to this mode of proof), but in its general harmony with scientific thought.

"And grotesque in relation to scientific culture as many of the religions of the world have been and are, — dangerous, nay, destructive, to the dearest privileges of freemen as some of them undoubtedly have been, and would, if they could, be again, — it will be wise to recognize them as the forms of a force, mischievous, if permitted to intrude on the region of *knowledge*, over which it holds no command, but capable of being guided to noble issues in the region of *emotion*, which is its proper and elevated sphere.

"All religious theories, schemes, and systems, which embrace notions of cosmogony, or which otherwise reach into the domain of Science, must, *in so far as they do this*, submit to the control of Science, and relinquish all thought of controlling it."

Religion does not wish or need to control Science, neither does it expect to be controlled by it. It is willing to go hand in hand with "Truth" at all times. Science has a right to know the principles of religious teachers and Religion, and Humanity demands the same in return from Science. In some respects we can renounce the past, its Science and Religion, but we have the present, and thus the inevitable future before us to live for.

The human mind, in whatever profession or calling it may be found, existent and ever enlarging under such influences as characterize the present age, naturally craves and seeks the truth. And for these reasons mankind are not willing, as in past generations, to rely upon the experiences and illustrations of others. Each for himself desires to see and weigh the foundations of asserted truth, as well as to draw conclusions from the relations of that truth to other things.

There was a seeming unity in the astronomical theories of all nationalities, up to the latest periods of their development; and the knowledge handed down to us by these old astronomers is beneficial, even though their conceptions of the truth may have been vague and erroneous. The epitomized record that the ancients have given us of personal investigation, and their knowledge or imagination of the condition and structure of the heavenly bodies, as well as their views of the other physical sciences, is dry, obscure, and sometimes superstitious, — but useful, nevertheless, and worth reading occasionally while we are making more practical observations on the same subjects in our own day. There is, moreover, a sublimity connected with some of their theories that carries the mind back and upward with force and beauty, proving the theory that man has within himself the germ of progress, in whatever sphere he may chance to be born.

Were he to attempt to harmonize this in his own career with modern science in all its bearings, sociology and evolution would forever go hand in hand in the inauguration of measures for human improvement and development. In the material objects around him he will see the workings of a high spiritual entity, that will point him upward and onward to the accomplishment of life's highest duties. In the physical sciences, his mind will at once soar from the material to the spiritual, and by retrospection influence all the stages of actienic evolution, to the creation of a globe or central sun. The resultant elements, with all their multiple principles and forces, will be pictured to him. Action and ether, electricity and magnetism, gravity, oxygen, hydrogen, nitrogen, all the gases, heat and cold, light and shade, atmosphere, vapor, material matter, nebulæ — an earth ! — in all these elements, and in their classification and association, their uses and possibilities, he will recognize sympathetic mental parallelisms whose union in their practical application gives him a study in which pleasure will ever unite with duty.

Says the Rev. J. Freeman Clarke, " Take away from the domain of knowledge the idea of a creating and presiding intelligence, and there remains no motive for Science itself. Professor Tyndall is sagacious enough to see and candid enough to admit that ' without moral force to whip it into action the achievements of the intellect would be poor indeed,' and that ' Science itself not unfrequently derives motive power from ultra-scientific sources.' Faith in God, as an intelligent Creator and Ruler of the world, has awakened enthusiasm for scientific investigation among both the Aryan and the Semitic races.

" The purest and highest form of Monotheism is that of Christianity ; and in Christendom has Science made its largest progress. Not by martyrs for Science, but by martyrs for Religion, has the human mind been emancipated. Mr. Tyndall says of scientific freedom, ' We fought and won our battle even in the Middle Ages.' But the heroes of intellectual liberty have been the heroes of faith. Hundreds of thousands have died for a religious creed ; but how many have died for a scientific theory ? Luther went to Worms, and maintained his opinions there in defiance of the anathemas of the Church and the ban of the empire; but Galileo denied his most cherished convictions on his knees. Galileo was as noble a character as Luther; but Science does not create the texture of soul which makes so many martyrs in all the religious sects of Christendom. It takes a sentimentalist like Gustavus Adolphus to die fighting for freedom of spirit. Let the doctrine of cosmical force supplant our faith in the Almighty, and in a few hundred years science would probably fade out of the world from pure inanition. The world would probably not care enough for *anything* to care for science. The light of eternity must fall on this, our human and earthly life, to arouse the soul to a living and permanent interest even in things seen and temporal." *

The " London Spectator" of August 22, in speaking of Professor Tyndall's Address, says, " True, matter needs other and wider definitions than it has yet received, definitions less mechanical, and according it wider range ; but still it is matter, and, as we conclude from the tone of the entire lecture, in Professor Tyndall's opinion, self-existent. Any cause for matter is an inference, a guess, which no scientific man is warranted making. Life and reason, as well as their instruments, have their origin in matter, the idea of a separate and immortal reason or soul being, on the whole, inadmissible, though on this point Professor Tyndall — who puts this division of his view into the form of a wonderfully eloquent dialogue between

---

* Galaxy, December, 1874, page 835.

Bishop Butler and a disciple of Lucretius — admits, or seems to admit, a mystery beyond which may lie somewhat of which the human understanding is too feeble to take cognizance. This, however, even if Professor Tyndall really allows so much, is but far off and unsupported conjecture; and the teaching of his whole lecture is that, so far as Science can ascertain, matter — expanding that word to include force as one of its attributes — is the final cause. Religion is but man's creation, though, as the desire for religion is one of the inherent forces of the mind, the gratification of that desire, so long as that gratification does not interfere with the paramount claim of Science to be free, may often be not only injurious, but highly beneficial.

"Plainer speaking than this can no man desire, and we need not say we have no quarrel with Mr. Tyndall for the plainness of his speech. We rather honor him for the courage which impels him to tell out his real thought, and face whatever of obloquy now attaches — and though little, it is often bitter — to opinions so extreme. If Materialism — we use the word without endorsing the opprobrium it is supposed to convey — is true, why waste time and energy and character in teaching what we know, or at least believe, to be so false? That practice can lead only to a restriction of intellectual effort, or to an intellectual hypocrisy even worse in its effects than hypocrisy as to morals. That the result of such a philosophy, if universally accepted, would be evil, or, rather, to avoid theological terminology, would be injurious to human progress, we have no doubt; but if it be true, the injury is no argument against its diffusion; for the injury, whatever its amount, is less than that which must proceed from the deliberate lying of the wise, or from the existence of that double creed, an exoteric and an esoteric one, which is the invariable result of their silence, or their limitation of speech to a circle of the initiated. Lucretius denying God and deifying Nature is a safer as well as nobler teacher than the Augur, chuckling in silent scorn as he announces to the mob the imaginary will of the gods whom, for him and for them alike, he believes to be non-existent. The evil the Professor will do arises not from any fault of his, — save so far as there may be moral fault in accepting such conclusions, a point upon which his conscience, and no other man's, must judge, — but from the cowardly subservience to authority which marks some would-be students of science as strongly as ever it marked any student of theology. There is a class of men among us who are in matters of science as amenable to authority as ever were ultramontanes, and who will accept a decision from Professor Tyndall, that the final cause is matter, just as readily and with just as complete a surrender of the right of private judgment as Catholics show when a pope decides that usury is immoral, or as the Peculiar People show when they let their children die because St. James did not believe in the value of medical advice. If Professor Tyndall affirmed that the final cause was heat, they would go about extolling the instinctive wisdom of the Guebres, and perhaps subscribe for a temple to maintain a perpetual fire. There will, however, be injury to such men; and if only for their sake, it would have been well if Professor Tyndall had, when announcing a conclusion which, if true, is fatal to all religion, — for thought evolved from matter is thought without responsibility, and man is necessarily sinless,— at all events stated frankly what his opponents would consider the great objections to his theory, had removed at least the primary difficulty, that the reference of all thought to motors apart from the independent and conceivably immortal mind in man, does not, like any other scientific assumption, explain the visible phenomena.

"The hypothesis does not, for instance, explain in any way the consciousness of free will, which is as strong as that consciousness of existence without which it is impossible to reason; or the independent influence of will, whether free or not, on the brain itself; or, above all, the existence of conflicting thoughts, going on in the mind at the same indivisible point of time. If a consciousness which is universal and permanent is not to be accepted as existing, why should the evidence of the senses, or the decision of reason, or the conclusions of science, be accepted either? If the fact, as we should call it, is mere illusion, why is not the evidence for the conservation of energy mere illusion too? Belief in either can only be the result of experience, and the experience as to the one is at least as great as the experience as to the other. Yet as the outcome of material forces, of any clash of atoms, any active relation between the organism and its environments, must be inevitable free will and thought evolved from machinery could not co-exist. The machine may be as fine as the mind can conceive, but still it can only do its natural work — cannot change its routine, cannot, above all, decline to act, as the mind unquestionably often consciously does. Lucretius, who killed himself to avoid corrupt imaginings, could, had his sanity been perfect, have controlled them, that is, could have declined to let the mind act as it was going to act; and in that control is at least an apparent demonstration that he possessed something above the product of any material energies. Professor Tyndall will say that animals show the same will; the dog, for instance, restraining the inclination to snap at food, though his mind, as you can see in his eyes, wants it as much as his body; but what new difficulty does that involve?

"Immortality for animals, says Bishop Butler, when he met that dilemma; and Professor Tyndall accepts that conclusion as only logical; but where is the logic that requires it? There is no objection that we know of, except prejudice, to the immortality of animals high enough in the scale to receive the separate reason, but neither is there any necessity why their separate reason should be deathless or incapable of absorption. The free will of man does not prove or involve immortality, which must be defended on quite other grounds, though it does prove the existence in man of a force not emanating from material sources. Professor Tyndall says if there were such a separate reason it could not be suspended or thrown into a trance, as it were by an external accident, but he does not prove that it is.

His argument from surgical experience — the apparent suspense of all faculties because a bone presses the brain — only shows that the relation between the soul — to employ the theological and best known term — and its instrument may be suspended for a time, but does not prove that the soul ceases even temporarily to be. The electric fluid exists even when the wire which conveys it ceases to be insulated. His moral illustration is stronger, because it carries us to the edge of the region where thought and experience alike begin to fail, but it is not conclusive."

The Editor of Harper's "New Monthly Magazine," in speaking of the subject (page 132), says: —

"Whatever may be thought of the soundness of the reasoning or the value of the conclusions in Professor Tyndall's Belfast Address, the important point to the present purpose is that it was the President of the British Association who spoke, and that his eminent position in Science is conceded. The essential interest of his Address is not so much its conclusions, as the fact that it was itself an assertion of what Roger Williams proudly called 'soul liberty.' Mr. Tyndall's real position was that, being quite as familiar with the methods and processes of life as other scientific or ecclesiastical scholars, he had a right to an opinion upon its origin, and an equal right to express his opinion. That he did so with eloquence and force, and with the respectful attention of able and scholarly thinkers, is another proof of that intellectual fidelity and independence which, despite every kind and degree of conformity and snobbery, still distinguish England, and justify the praise of her laureate : —

> " ' It is the land that freemen till,
> That sober-suited Freedom chose;
> The land where, girt with friends or foes,
> A man may speak the thing he will.' "

ESSAY XI.

SEISMIC AND MENTAL ENERGIES.

The written history of the world, whether considered in a physical or metaphysical sense, has taught man very little compared with what he has learned from the practical study of cause and effect. The geological investigation of the crusts of the earth has enabled him, from close examination and tracings of its metamorphic strata and versatile composition, to reason back to the causes which gave those telluric lamina existence in their present shape. The masses of siliceous matter, bones, and other fossils and deposits of which the strata are largely made up, and its known alternate rendings, tossings, and submersions, with the chemical and integral changes that obviously must follow, give us a good idea of the secondary causes of its condition at the present time.

Had the seismic forces not existed, which have so metamorphosed the globe, or, existing, had not worked as they have, we should to-day enjoy a very different world in its electric, hydrometric, and atmospheric sense, and know much less concerning its probable molecular and atomic origin. We have been similarly educated through the impact and vibration of terrestrial atmospheric energies, as well as by the examination of fluid, vaporous, and gaseous elements around and above us. The constituencies of ponderable and imponderable ever-changing substances with which we have grown familiar, existing above us, and gliding beneath our feet at every tread, have given us conceptions of the actienic and etheric primal forces from which all more material matter may consistently emanate. This gives scope for argument on two of the extreme theories of mental and physical creation which are now under continuous debate, the one having a *material* and the other an *ethereal* basis.

We believe that the spiritual and ethereal idea has precedence, and when fully developed will prove the origin of all ponderable substance; and if not identical with our previously conceived notions, will, no doubt, be as novel and wonderful, if not more sublime and useful, than our wildest imaginings could picture. These two opposing principles or theories have been antagonistically embraced by different scientific writers of the present day, who, if they do not convince, are certainly enlightening the world with their research and learning.

We believe in science as well as in religion, and we believe also that they do not and need not conflict; but that from the most dense material, fluid, gaseous, or imponderable matter, onward through every evolution to Deity itself, there is spiritual and mental revelation to man, which becomes daily and hourly nourishment and sustenance to body, intellect, and mind. In some generations the Church has monopolized a great part of the learning of the day, but in such case religion or worship was the more material, — true spiritual elevation remaining in the background. The study of science, then, should be also the study of religion, which is its life and duty, lighting their pathway onward and upward to the author of all — God.

The Dark Ages held for a time a thick curtain over the past, which was raised under a new order of things, unfortunately, however, to find human progress still subjected to the hinderances ever interposed by the selfishness and jealousies of human nature. These at present almost inseparable constituents, in the new as well as in the old order of things, gave rise again to dogmatism, arrogance, Saddusaic opinionism, and monkish fanaticism, — which spirit still unfortunately, to a limited extent, pervades and retards material, mental, and spiritual progress. Had it not been so, perchance knowledge would have been precipitated too fast for the proper digestion and practical use of man and the highest development of his better nature, as indicated by the new impulse of life given to his increasing strength and moral growth.

Before this great change, the races, with all their former prestige of physical and intellectual strength, seemed gone to decay, — a seeming death, only to be followed by a new birth, and a greater, higher work, in succeeding centuries, when Science shall not be divorced from Literature or Religion, when Spiritual life shall not be ignored by Materialism; but rather that a greater and broader comprehension of the laws of nature shall reveal to every soul in its sphere a higher existence, a universal, spiritual sympathy for the whole laws of God.

"And now," says Professor Tyndall, "the end is come. With more time, or greater strength and knowledge, what has been here said might have been better said, while worthy matters here omitted might have received fit expression. But there would have been no material deviation from the views set forth. As regards myself, they are not the growth of a day; and as regards you, I thought you ought to know the environment which, with or without your consent, is rapidly surrounding you, and in relation to which some adjustment on your part may be necessary. A hint of Hamlet's, however, teaches us all how the troubles of common life may be ended; and it is perfectly possible for you and me to purchase intellectual peace at the price of intellectual death. The world is not without refuges of this description, nor is it wanting in persons who seek their shelter and try to persuade others to do the same. The unstable and the weak will yield to this persuasion, and they to whom repose is sweeter than the truth. But I would exhort you to refuse the offered shelter and to scorn the base repose, — to accept, if the choice be forced upon you, commotion before stagnation, the leap of the torrent before the stillness of the swamp."

The end is not yet, say the tens of thousands who have read Professor Tyndall's Address. An issue which has stirred all Christendom has been raised between Science and Religion by the President of the British Association. That issue is still being weighed by thousands who look upon it as approaching very near the sanctuary of their spiritual and material rest. It is not that they wish to deny Science or

Professor Tyndall any privileges, but that they feel that his doctrine, if well intentioned, will be misunderstood. The most sympathetic of critics say this. They do not wish to brand him as an atheist; yet, when ten lines of his pen would set the matter right before the world, they cannot help doubting the possibility of his allegiance to a Deity that he clouds with doubt.

This would lead us to the consideration of the changes, by physical transformations, of our globe since its beginning, which must have been no less wonderful than the changes in animate life, whether we reason from its lowest order, or from mankind of historic times.

Human progress has kept pace with the revelations of the past, as well as with the unfoldings of the present time. The history of ancient scientific research has been amended in most cases by new and forcible practical illustrations. Astronomy, as understood by the ancients, becomes illumined by the discoveries of the present day, and the most distant empires are rapidly made acquainted with the progress of the sciences in Europe and America. Their philosophers are in communication with our own scientists, and report to their respective peoples the more rapid progress of Christian nationalities.

Thales, Pythagoras, Ptolemy, Plato, and Aristotle did their work and served their age, giving place to Purbach, Copernicus, Tycho-Brahe, Kepler, Galileo, Newton, and Herschel, who, in turn, bequeathed the treasures of their patient gleanings to more modern astronomers.

The mental energies and revelations of our own day have been more general and diffusive, through increasing liberalism, than those of the past, and all the sciences now form each an integral portion of one great whole. The universe is studied by scientists of all professions, and the stellar world is being grasped as in a span, and yearly opens something instructively new to our vision of the great truths of creation, as well as the mysteries of etheric space.

The sun, through the progress of mental action, is being clothed with new theoretic garbs by spectroscopic investigation, throwing off the old theories that for a century have been growing threadbare under the watchful yet feeble eye of the more tardy telescopic examination. It seems no longer certain that this orb is a molten mass, uninhabited, and unfitted for man.

The planets increase yearly on our maps and charts, and many of the old ideas of their physical condition have been laid aside, and new and more practical ones have been substituted.

The electric and magnetic evolutions of our atmosphere, and its humid and thermometric conditions, are being better understood every day. Light and heat find new, additional, and more practical support in the actinic and etheric theories of combustion of molecular substance, and the laws of evolution qualify motors of projection and force, in mental as well as physical energies.

The theories of Humboldt, Herschel, and others in regard to auroral and zodiacal lights have been modified by the spectroscopic analysis, giving place in part to actienic combustion; and the polar sea, the pole of cold, and the magnetic circle have place in the probable estimates of scientific truths of the present day. The electric telegraph practically surrounds the globe, and the steam-engine is doing the work of man and muscle. The products of the earth are enlarging day by day, and the mind of man, it is hoped, keeps pace with its own accruing advantages of sociology. The theory daily grows stronger that the stellar and solar systems, and all matter, whether solid, fluid, or gaseous, electricity, magnetism, the atmosphere, and all molecular substance, were originally created by, through, and from the action of two primary and negative principles in space.

That the sun, as the centre and primary origin of the solar system, through actienic forces, sends off its wavy, pointed rays to the planets of its creation, in general undulatory straight lines, not necessarily heated or luminous on leaving the sun, but becoming so on passing through space and penetrating the atmosphere of the planet and entering into combustion with it, giving light and heat as a result.

That light and heat, as such, do not to any great extent emanate from the sun, and that the sun's heat does not extend beyond its own atmosphere; the apparent light and heat of the sun, as seen and felt upon the earth, being caused by actienic rays flowing from the sun to the earth through the ether of space, and which by friction and combustion with ether and the atmosphere by wave crests, causes the creation of the light and heat enjoyed on the surface of the earth.

That electricity and magnetism are the products of actienic and etheric combustion, followed by the gases, atmosphere, light, heat, cold, vapor, water, the solids, etc.

That light and color, heat and cold, are conditions, and not principles.

That there are seeming principles contradictory of recognized laws, such as weight and attraction, opposing gravity, evaporation, and congelation inconsistent with the thermal conditions usually controlling these processes.

That caloric and absolute heat must be even lighter than the surrounding atmosphere of lower temperature, and will flow upward but not downward through the same.

That the present recognized theory of heat and light of the solar system cannot be correct, and that an imponderable fluid, neither heated nor luminous, supplies both these wants.

That the magnetic currents are naturally terrestrial, while the electric are more celestial; and that the former produces in the earth conflicts and explosions, as the latter does in the clouds above.

That the magnetic pole is a circle instead of a point, as also a pole of cold.

That the auroral and zodiacal lights are actienic and electric.

That there must be an open polar sea of great depth, and that tides are only controlled, not caused, by the attractions of the sun and moon; but rather are caused by the change of the attractive points in the revolution of the earth, passing the focal line of motion every six hours, which necessarily turns the current back.

That unfixed or atmospheric colors were governed by the particular angle upon which the light struck the plates of atmosphere through which they pass, and impinge the overlapping, crossing, or vapor-loaded strata of the air above and around us.

That cold or heat would change the electric and magnetic currents without transmitting their own essence, as also effecting light and color, and that the form of crystallization of solid matter in the same would control the color by fixing the refracting angle upon which the light would strike it.

That the planets, by the actienic powers of combustion, would be supplied by a uniform quantity of light and heat approximate to their sphere, whatever their distance, and in such form as to render the nearest or most distant planet from the sun habitable.

That heat cannot be strictly latent as such, but being a condition must be at all times operative.

That the actienic or etheric properties may pervade all matter and molecular substance, itself lying dormant or in a normal condition, without showing any temperature of heat but by compression, percussion, or friction, the dormant fluids going into combustion, creating heat. If such combustion were in a transparent element there would also be light, but if hidden within opaque walls it would show only heat.

That the actienic and etheric forces are compensative in all their relations of evolution, passing through all the phases from inponderable to ponderable matter, thence retracing the ground to imponderable again, but not in sense of igneous combustion.

Our existence, to be conscious, furnishes its own proof of birth and connection with physical matter, yet the very knowledge of such being brings with it the further evidence that the material part of life is evanescent and dying, while the spiritual is living and growing.

"Spirit" must ever be considered the primate and the ultimate,— the beginning and end of all power, goodness, and greatness, reaching everywhere and pervading all things, yet centred in and radiating from God alone.

Science, unemotional, cold, and calculating, may approach the very footstool of its throne, examine, criticise, and appropriate the lights and shadows of its entity, as the molecular causality of material substance; but Religion alone, the soul of Science, can penetrate, see, feel, and drink in the gleams of its divine existence.

Science is the skeleton of atomic construction; Religion is the life, the soul of its human development; Prayer, the thermometric oscillations of mental force, projecting the spirit of man sympathetically upward to the sanctuary of its Author.

ESSAY XII.

CREATION OF THE UNIVERSE.

An impulse of Deity, inherent through its own entity, created and inspired the world of spirit. These conscious, dual life-energies, still impelled under a Divine will, moved in space, and two imponderable primary forces, with positive and negative poles, were created. The impact of these opposing principles produced molecules, both ponderable and imponderable, as a result, — the imponderable taking their place in the higher forms of ethereal development, such as electricity, magnetism, and of life-forces; and the ponderable, the more physical creations of atomic substance. Molecules embodying positive and negative forces war with each other. These, ever acting within the influence of all subsequent creations of life-force, — their subdivisions and mechanical combinations constantly moving, — make life and matter progressive through all forms of evolution; and thus, these two primary principles obeying the natural impulse given at the hand of Deity, unite, change, or recombine their molecular energies in the generation of other positive and negative forces, secondary to their own, which in like manner attract one another, change, or re-combine again, —

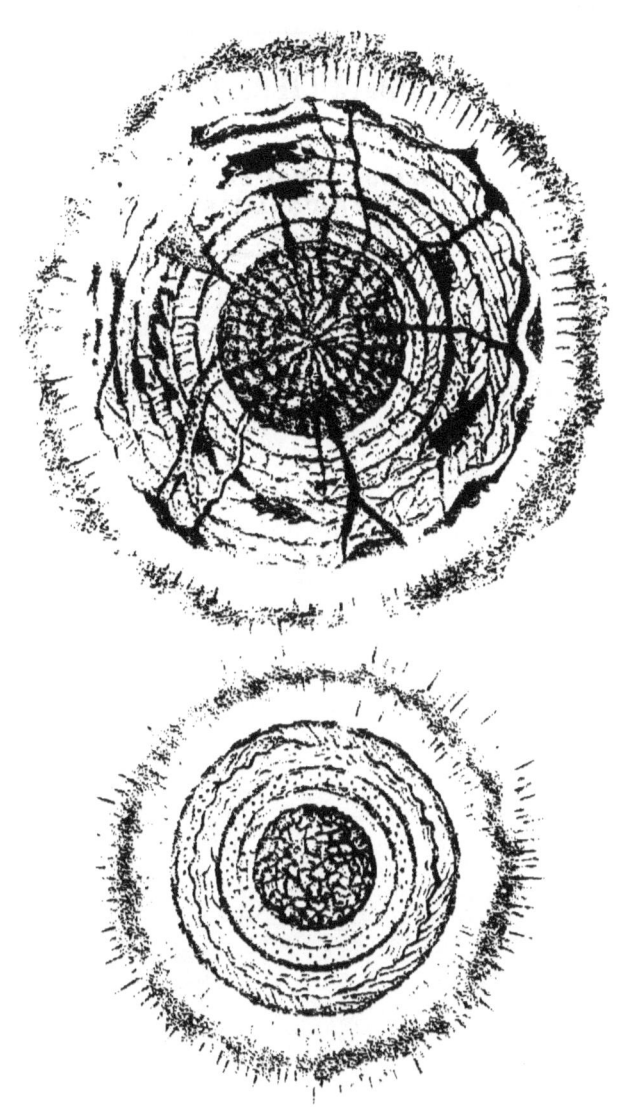

THE NEW YORK
PUBLIC LIBRARY

ASTOR, LENOX AND
TILDEN FOUNDATIONS

CREATION OF THE UNIVERSE. 169

and so moving onward, all imponderable elements of which we have any knowledge, with their peculiar attractive or repulsive, as well as disintegrating and integrating powers, are brought into existence.

Again, these original principles, together with those imponderable substances of their creation, move forward in the march of evolution, and ponderable matter is produced. Material molecules are aggregated and combined; a ball of solid matter is formed, with gravity, properties of attraction and repulsion; atmosphere and vapor follow, surrounded and permeated by electric, magnetic, and other known principles, uniting, changing, and recombining in the birth of a miniature world, launched into existence and obeying the laws of motion, traversing in its orbit the realms of etheric space.

The law of change is incessant, — the moving ball is without rest; conflicting elements surround and clasp it; the globules of to-day become the falling rain-drops of to-morrow; the crust is softened and disintegrated; continued showers wash it away, through denudated channels, to unresisting deltas, where its momentary rest is again broken from the rockings and tossings of river currents or ocean waves.

Heat is generated around it; electric and magnetic currents charge its attractive powers; new chemical combinations follow at every hand; vegetation springs up from its bosom, siliceous and crustaceous strata of different forms issue, with its additional pressure, producing by its frictional force upon the naturally-laid molecules of matter, the heat of combustion.

Accumulations of the powers of weight, attractive force, more heat, an electric, magnetic, or gaseous explosion, and the crust is rent asunder, the deltas of rivers and the bottoms of oceans are raised, becoming dry land, while other valleys are made and some added to the already-existing water-bed.

The work goes on, Time always laughing at Nature and her increasing, changing forces; the strata are again upturned, while fertile valleys and flowery glens are buried beneath the deep, and there become beds of coral growth and saline floral plains.

Thus moves and thrives a world in its onward course, and glory of change and growth. Surplus energies arise, shoot forth from its attractive shell, escape the thrall, and rush into space, the actienic force for other worlds to build. Matter, ponderable and imponderable, revels unconscious in its war with matter till a dawn of new light appears.

Motion has new impulse — voluntary, locomote; the mist globules that arise from the mountain glen, or cling to ocean bed, obey no more the law that made them; new forces govern, an unknown power moves and holds them; it is ANIMAL LIFE! A living existence disputes the further independent creation by seismic energies alone. A new struggle begins and is kept in action; generative creations multiply the life-forces of an animate existence, which are pitted against the works of inanimate material matter. The struggle is great, the victory not decided, though the shell of earth becomes the crustacean mausoleum of departed life.

The mountains crumble to dust, the ocean bed is

CREATION OF THE UNIVERSE. 171

raised to breathe from conflict, and ages clothe in verdure that battle-ground of created matter. A new life dawns, higher, weightier than the last; and MAN, a human soul, appears.

New life, energy, force, method, and dominion appear on land and sea, on earth and in air, license to inhabit, use, and convert all that will aid his fellow-man and do honor to the Giver.

The birth of worlds has begun! Onward the march in regular line of orbit; order and system prevail; and worlds of matter and worlds of spirit float onward and upward at the call of Deity!

www.ingramcontent.com/pod-product-compliance
Lightning Source LLC
Chambersburg PA
CBHW020248170426
43202CB00008B/278